PENGUIN super

BOOK OF PHOTOGRAPHY

Peter MacDonald
Don Honeyman
Angelo Hornak

NEWNES BOOKS

Contents

This book was commissioned by Pentax U.K. Limited

Published by Newnes Books,
a Division of The Hamlyn Publishing Group Limited
84-88, The Centre, Feltham, Middlesex
and distributed for them by
The Hamlyn Publishing Group Limited
Rushden, Northants, England

Printed and bound by Graficromo s.a., Cordoba, Spain

Foreword

Photography is enjoyed by almost everyone, even if only in the passive sense that they would be less likely to pick up a newspaper or magazine if there were no photographs in it. It is true that few people can escape the influence of the printed picture for very long: it is everywhere.

The industry which supplies the insatiable appetite for visual records is massive—but it is, like all the great manufacturing industries, taken for granted. One day you may chance to see it in action, and you will be impressed. Try to visualise all those lenses rolling off the production lines, each one a compact marvel of applied optical technology, manufactured in the sterile atmosphere of the plant far away from the grimy world where it was designed to operate. Imagine the camera design offices where day after day the proportions of the human hand in all its variety and its anatomical sophistication are analysed, along with the arm, the eye and the whole physical aspect of camera use. Imagine the lightless environment in which photographic emulsions are coated on to mile after mile of transparent film base, issuing tons of film which, if it were all joined together, would come reeling out of the factory at the rate of hundreds of miles per hour. Then there is the developing and printing industry which turns out millions and millions of prints, good, bad and otherwise.

If you cannot take good pictures it is not because this industry is asleep or oblivious to your requirements. Those of us who make a living out of photography do not get special treatment. It is hard work. If you own a Pentax you can really enjoy the act of photographing, and with patience, application and the odd bit of luck, you can make pictures that will be a source of pleasure for many years.

Sam Haskins
South London, June 1982

Introduction

Numerous books on photography are available, devoted either to equipment and equipment purchasing, or to different aspects of the photographic art. The *Pentax ME Super Book of Photography* is designed to feature in one volume every relevant aspect of a highly popular single-lens reflex camera and its system, and provide a simple but effective guide to the photographic art.

Photography as a hobby and as a medium has grown spectacularly over the last decade, and in this volume it is our intention to maximize your use and enjoyment of this medium and the opportunities made available to you by the modern Pentax SLR.

How to use this book

Given the wide range of skills and experience that different photographers will bring to their new camera, it is inevitable that not all sections in this book will be of equal importance to everyone. The following summary should help you to find the information that will be of most interest or assistance to you personally.

Chapter 1 is an introduction to photographic principles and provides simplified descriptions of the processes, the materials and the equipment common to all forms of photography.

Chapters 2 and 3 plot the development of the single-lens reflex camera, explaining exactly why the design has proved so successful. The treatment of the subject is logical but not chronological, and is intended to help the user to understand all the functions of the modern SLR. If you understand these already, pass on to chapter 4 or chapter 6.

Chapters 4 and 5 are about Pentax cameras in particular. A comprehensive description of camera features and facilities is followed by a look at every model in the current Pentax range.

Chapters 6–8 describe the Pentax ME Super in detail, giving instructions for its use as both an automatic and a manual camera. These chapters form the nucleus of the publication and will be of interest to all owners of the ME Super.

Chapters 9 and 10 are about Pentax filters and electronic flash units.

Chapter 11 catalogues all current SMC Pentax lenses with a general introduction explaining the obvious and not-so-obvious reasons for changing lenses, and showing some of the surprising effects that may be obtained. This chapter is a must for anyone new to SLR photography.

Finally, chapter 12 is a lengthy self-contained section written by two professional photographers who between them have worked in every major subject area, and who give an enormous amount of practical advice about using the ME Super to take successful photographs.

There are also two full-colour sections of thirty-two pages each, containing ten carefully selected portfolios of colour photographs. These are beautiful portfolios in themselves, but they illustrate the use of many pieces of equipment and points of camera technique and are intended to be helpful as well as decorative.

1 Introduction to photographic principles

The opening sections of this book are intended for people who are new to photography and for those who have decided, perhaps after years of owning a camera and putting it to occasional use without a lot of thought, that the time has come to get a *real* camera and learn how to use it properly. More experienced photographers who have acquired one of the Pentax range of single-lens reflexes may prefer to turn straight to the practical sections beginning on page 177, or to study the colour portfolios found towards the end of the book.

But first things first. Even complete novices will naturally want to go out and use their new camera at the first opportunity. The instruction manual supplied with every new camera gives abbreviated operating instructions so that no more time than necessary need be lost in making it ready for use. The instructions are given in an expanded form in this book, starting on page 49.

At more leisure, however, you may find it profitable to look at the sections on light, photographic film, cameras and the evolution of the modern single-lens reflex. These are included because the experience of photographers of many different backgrounds and varying levels of ambition has shown that without an understanding of the medium and the materials they come sooner or later to a point where they are limited to admiring the work of others, rather than creating for themselves the kind of pictures that they want to see. This applies just as much to a set of holiday photographs as it does to a portfolio of artistic works. Most people already have an intuitive familiarity with light and the photographic process, but it does help if it is raised to the conscious level of the mind as a preliminary to making memorable photographs.

Light

Any light can be used to make photographs, but the types of photograph that can be made in any given conditions depend on

(i) the source
(ii) the intensity
(iii) the colour of the light.

Source

The sun is the original source of all natural light (except starlight, which in photography is of only limited relevance) but in practice the sun's rays never reach the surface of the earth without being altered. This complicates matters to a surprising extent. In fact, the ways in which sunlight is altered are so dramatic that for photographic purposes it cannot be treated as a single source at all: it is a number of quite distinct sources, all powered by the same generator.

Direct sun Light travels outwards in straight lines from its source, becoming ever less concentrated, and therefore dimmer, as its illumination expands unimpeded into space. It is direct if its rays are unaltered by any other agent at a given point. Direct light will illuminate the near side of an opaque object and leave the far side in total darkness. An illustration of

These two photographs of an old log cart show how different light can be on different days. In the top picture, direct summer sun has maximized contrast; a much softer result was obtained on an overcast autumn day.

direct natural light that is familiar to everybody is provided by the moon, which actually appears to change its shape in the course of a lunar month because to the unaided eye its dark side is indistinguishable from the blackness beyond. Here on earth, direct light can be created artificially but *it never occurs alone in nature* because some of it is always scattered in the atmosphere and only reaches us *in*directly (hence our luminous blue skies, rather than the inky black ones that appear in outer space).

But direct light can be the dominant component of mixed daylight: when the orb of the sun itself is visible during the middle hours of a clear day its rays are strong and highly directional. Surfaces on the sunward side of an object are brilliantly lit; those on the shaded side appear dense and black, and the line that divides light from shade is sharp and well defined.

Skylight Even on cloudless days the sun's aggressive intensity is diluted: some wavelengths are scattered by the atmosphere, so that the entire bowl of the sky from horizon to horizon acts as an immense panel of even blue light. Over the region as a whole, direct sunlight and skylight are mixed: localities that are shielded from direct sunlight, e.g. by mountains or tall buildings, are illuminated by skylight alone. Not emanating from a point source, skylight is diffused, or non-directional, and does not cast hard shadows of its own. To an observer standing in it, the shadow seems less dense than it does to another observer standing at a vantage point in full sun and looking into it; this is because the former's eyes are not affected by the brilliance of the sun which he cannot see.

Diffused sun Water vapour in the form of mist, fog or clouds of various kinds, and smoke, dust and other pollutants can all occur independently or together in the atmosphere. As they accumulate or disperse they have the effect of progressively attenuating or boosting the intensity and directness of sunlight. Conditions may alter unpredictably all day long or they may stabilize at any point on the scale between full sun casting hard shadows, through thin high cloud and thick low cloud to an engulfing fog. For photographic purposes, clouds, whether occurring singly or in layers, can be considered light sources in themselves. An even layer of bright cloud that covers the sky provides lighting that is exactly adapted to the light-recording capacity of ordinary photographic films.

Reflected daylight Whatever its primary source, when light strikes a solid surface other than a matt black one some of it is reflected, and the reflecting surface must occasionally be considered as a source of usually low, diffused, and sometimes coloured light. Often reflected light of this kind can be disregarded because it is swamped by more powerful sources. But sometimes it is very important. Domestic interiors, for example, are often lit by a single window, it being the light reflected back and forth around the room that illuminates the corners from which no window can be seen. In cases like this it is more helpful to consider the walls and other surfaces as the light source, and not just the window itself. This is particularly so if the walls are brightly coloured.

It is reflected light, of course, that tells us about the physical world by giving shape, texture and colour to the objects in it: more about this later.

Artificial sources Depending on the resources available, artificial light may be direct or diffused, of any intensity and any colour. This makes it rather a specialized subject.

Intensity

To be able to measure accurately the intensity or quantity of light delivered by any source is of fundamental importance in photography. Everybody knows that light may be strong or weak, but some of the statistics may come as a surprise.

Take as a starting point the minimum amount of light required to activate the light meter built into the ME Super and MX cameras: as the meter is highly sensitive this minimum is very low indeed—maybe less than that on a landscape by moonlight. Let us ascribe a nominal value to this quantity of light: say, 1. Now let this value increase by 1 each time the amount of light is doubled. By the time we get to the figure 19, which is the upper end of the ME Super's metering capability, that original quantity of light will have been increased by a factor of 262144—in other words the brightest light that it can measure is over a quarter of a million times as bright as the dimmest.

The human eye is sensitive to major variations in the intensity of light,

In an interior lit by natural light, overall illumination is low; but the human eye soon becomes acclimatized and sees normally within a few moments.

Outside in harsh sunlight the overall illumination may be hundreds or thousands of times greater, but we often do not really notice the difference.

but not to relatively small fluctuations: it is equipped with an iris diaphragm that closes down or opens up in response to such changes, and this cushions the brain against shocks so that light may halve, or double, or even quadruple in intensity without our being made aware of it. We know that a domestic interior lit at night by general service bulbs is not as bright as the garden on a sunny afternoon; what the eye cannot tell us, and a light meter can, is that the interior light in the former scene measures perhaps 6 on the scale while the sunlight in the latter is closer to 13—which is 128 times as much light. That is quite a difference, when you think about it.

To get good photographs, you must regulate the intensity of the light so that it matches the sensitivity of the film in the camera and nothing can be finely regulated if it has not been accurately measured in the first place.

Colour composition

When evaluating light for photographic purposes, a good number of inexperienced photographers consider *only* its intensity. Accurate measurement of this is a prerequisite if pictures are to be obtained at all with an adjustable camera, but light has another property which affects the appearance of the finished photographs: its spectral composition, or more loosely, its colour.

If the human eye and brain are quite tolerant of changes in the intensity of light, they are downright insensitive when it comes to changes in its colour composition. This is an asset in everyday life, but it is an enemy of good colour photography, particularly with reversal films.

White light is composed of all the colours of the spectrum, as every schoolchild knows. But pure white light is seldom encountered except under laboratory conditions. Daylight and most forms of artificial light vary in colour according to all sorts of factors, and although this usually goes unnoticed in everyday life, photographs bearing a particular colour cast are very readily rejected by the mind as being the 'wrong' colour. Specific examples are photographs taken by ordinary household lighting, which is actually orange-red in colour; those taken by fluorescent light, which is greenish; those taken in the open shade, where the prevailing skylight may be bluish in colour; and those taken in the evening around sunset, when the light is yellow-orange-red in hue.

These problems can be overcome by the use of coloured filters over the lens, or by careful selection of film, or a combination of both; but the problem has to be identified before it can be solved, and the tolerance of the eye makes this very difficult. The use of a colour temperature meter (which analyses the spectral composition of the light and indicates what film/filter combination will give a neutral result) is the best solution, but this is an expensive and specialized accessory. A more workable compromise is to use the standard colour-correction filters.

Naturally it is not always necessary or desirable to correct the colour bias imparted to a subject by a particular kind of light. Some subjects just look insipid in their own neutral colours, and it can be an improvement to leave or even exaggerate the effects of coloured light. But throughout this book the emphasis is on the control that modern materials and equipment offer the photographer. By all means create strange and lurid colour effects if you want to, but let them be what you *chose* to make them, not an accident that happened because you missed something.

Film

The structure of black and white film

Photographic film is a flexible transparent material coated on one side with a layer of gelatin. Evenly distributed within the gelatin layer or 'emulsion' are billions of microscopic crystals called silver salts or halides. These particles are light-sensitive: that is, when in contact with light they undergo a rapid physical change. It is on this property that the whole photographic process is founded.

How photographs are made

The lens of a camera projects on to this film an image of the world outside. Although permitted to do so only for a brief period—usually only a fraction of a second—enough light falls on the silver halides to alter their physical structure. Large crystals are readily altered and small ones less so, and as the emulsion contains crystals of different sizes mixed at random, the average degree of change over any given area depends on the local intensity of the light that the lens has transmitted.

The alteration in the structure of the crystals is too slight to be visible to the human eye, and has to be boosted by a two-stage chemical process which consists of (i) converting the affected crystals to black metallic silver, or 'developing' the film, and (ii) dissolving and removing all the rest, 'fixing' the film, so that what is left is a pattern of microscopic black dots on a clear film base. When this is held against a light source a negative image can be seen: that is, brightness of the original is represented by darkness in the negative image, and vice versa. To correct this reversal the negative image is 'printed'—rephotographed on to a fresh emulsion which has opaque white paper as a base. After processing in the same way as before, the monochromatic print emerges.

The basic process – a negative image is formed of the subject as described in the text, and then the camera has done its job; the rest is up to the processors and printers.

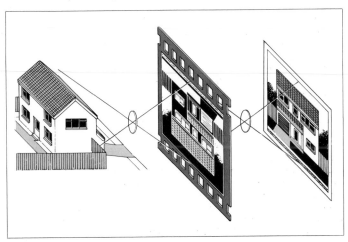

Colour film

The structure of colour films is naturally more complex than that of black and white film, but the same principle is utilized. In effect, three latent images are formed instead of a single one, each on a separate layer of emulsion. In the pioneering days of photography three photographs were taken separately through filters, but advances in technology have made it possible economically to produce emulsions which respond selectively to light in different parts of the spectrum. These are all coated on to the same film base.

Each of the emulsion layers is sensitive to one of the primary colours, and depending on their relative densities they can combine to make an image of any colour and tone. In addition to rendering visible the latent images, the successive stages in processing also convert them to the correct colour. If the film is of the reversal type, for making transparencies which are viewed by transmitted light, the actual colours of the original are generated, and the finished picture emerges direct from the developing tank. Colour negatives from which prints are to be made emerge in complementary colours, and these are subsequently rephotographed on to sheets of sensitized paper, which then bear a colour positive image.

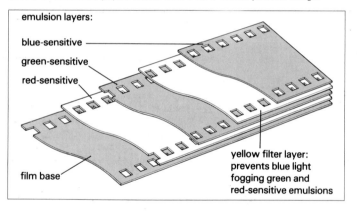

emulsion layers:

blue-sensitive

green-sensitive

red-sensitive

film base

yellow filter layer: prevents blue light fogging green and red-sensitive emulsions

The structure of colour film: it consists of a 'tripack', or three-layer gelatin coating with an additional filter layer.

Film speed

An important quality of both colour and monochromatic films is known as 'speed'. A fast film is one which is highly sensitive to light and therefore takes up an image very rapidly; a slow film is less sensitive and needs a longer period of exposure to the light. Thus, given the same camera settings, a fast film can take up an image in much dimmer conditions than a slow one. This difference is based on the size of the crystals in the emulsion. As we have seen, the large crystals react more readily than the small ones, which is what gives the negative image its tone. If the average size is large, the emulsion as a whole takes up the image more readily than if the average size is small. The advantage of speed must, however, be

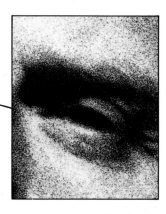

The detail from a print that was already greatly enlarged clearly shows the granular structure of the photographic image.

weighed against the relative coarseness of the grain—the particles of black metallic silver that make up the negative image—which at high magnifications can show loss of detail.

Different scales are in use to express film speed. With the ASA system, which is the one used on Pentax equipment, a doubling of the number represents a doubling of film speed: 400 ASA is twice as fast as 200 ASA, which is twice as fast as 100 ASA, and so on. With the DIN system a doubling of film speed is indicated by the addition of 3; thus 400, 200 and 100 ASA are the same as 27, 24 and 21 DIN respectively. Other systems – Weston, GOST, ISO and others – are in existence, but it is simpler to get used to one system and stay with it.

Where image quality must be put before all else, slow films (less than 100 ASA) should be chosen; but normally medium to fast films (up to 400 ASA) are perfectly adequate for most photographic purposes and they allow greater flexibility of exposure.

The camera

Light is the medium, film is the material. The camera is the instrument that is designed to bring the two together in an organized way in order to make photographs. The process is simple in principle, and any apparent complication stems from the degree of refinement to which it has been subjected.

The camera consists of a box which admits no light except through a small hole in the front. This opening is equipped with (i) a lens that projects into the back of the box an image of the scene in front of it, and (ii) an opening and closing mechanism called a shutter. When released the shutter springs open for a fixed period, e.g. 1/50 second, and the film at the back of the camera box is exposed. It is then processed as described earlier.

All modern cameras, however sophisticated, are developed from this embryonic form, and whatever else they may have, they must always have a lens, a shutter mechanism and a lightproof casing.

How a lens gathers light

Light travels in straight lines until it encounters a solid object; and air, glass, water, people, metal — in fact anything that can be seen — are all more or less 'solid' in that light cannot pass straight through them unimpeded. On meeting one of these substances light may be redirected (by reflection and/or refraction) or absorbed. In practice both usually happen together, but in what proportions depends on the properties of the surface.

All surfaces except matt black ones reflect at least some of the light that falls on them and absorb the rest. It is the quantity and spectral composition of the light they reflect that gives them their distinguishing characteristics: according to quantity we call a surface dull or bright; according to its spectral composition we attribute a colour to it, and these are the factors that give what we perceive as form, substance and colour to the physical world.

When light strikes any point of a matt surface its reflected component explodes off in many directions at once (which is how it becomes 'visible' from all around) so that an environment cluttered with objects of all shapes, sizes and colours — e.g. the earth's surface — is constantly bombarded with light of all densities and qualities, from every direction, reflected and re-reflected in a turbulent but highly organized bedlam of visual sensations

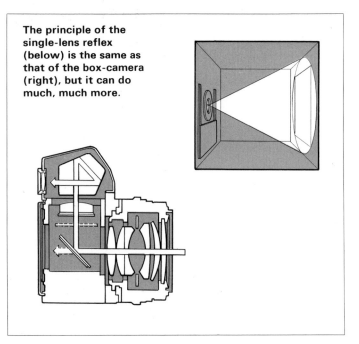

The principle of the single-lens reflex (below) is the same as that of the box-camera (right), but it can do much, much more.

—like millions upon millions of people all furiously playing ping-pong on the same small table.

The lens of a camera, like that of the eye, receives over its entire surface light emanating from every point in the world before it. As the rays from any given point pass through the lens they are refracted, or bent, so that instead of continuing to spread out they converge again, finally coming to a point, or 'focus' on the other side. As long as the photographic film is situated in the plane of focus a precise image of the subject will be formed on the film when the exposure is made.

In fact, lenses do not work as simply as this, a fact which has led to the development of intricate compound lenses such as those described in more detail in chapter 11.

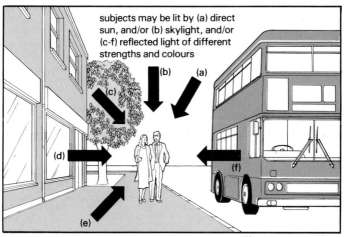

subjects may be lit by (a) direct sun, and/or (b) skylight, and/or (c-f) reflected light of different strengths and colours

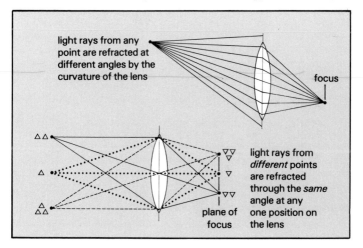

light rays from any point are refracted at different angles by the curvature of the lens

focus

light rays from *different* points are refracted through the *same* angle at any one position on the lens

plane of focus

2 The modern camera and its controls

Though primitive, the box-camera described at the end of the previous chapter can be a highly efficient unit. It works well provided that (i) the subject is neither too close to the camera nor too far away; (ii) there is bright daylight available for photography; (iii) the subject is not moving at any great speed; (v) the user will not need to work fast or in difficult circumstances, and, less obvious but very important in advanced photography, that (v) he will never need to vary the angle of view that the fixed lens is designed to give. There are other limitations too, but these are the major ones.

When any one or more of these conditions is not met, either image quality becomes seriously degraded, or the act of photographing becomes difficult if not impossible.

The history of camera design is one of a relentless striving for improvement, for ways of extending the performance limits of existing systems without sacrificing simplicity of operation. Advances do not occur in isolation: they are the products of a process of organic growth, each step forward in one area of camera design providing a new platform for research and experimentation in others. In the interests of clarity, focusing and exposure controls are treated separately in the descriptions that follow; their evolution and functions are, however, indivisibly connected.

Focusing lenses

A lens like the one illustrated on page 15 cannot be adjusted to bring into focus objects immediately in front of the camera. This is not so much a restriction imposed by the optical properties of the glass element itself (although these may play a part); the governing factor is the lack of any mechanical means of varying the distance between the lens and the film plane.

Theoretically, light from any single point in front of the lens is brought to a focus *somewhere* behind it. Light rays from a distant point are almost parallel when they enter the lens, so that after refraction they converge rapidly and come to a focus a short distance behind it. The rays from a nearby point are diverging when they strike the perimeter of the lens, so that although they are refracted through the same angle as the light from any other point, they converge only slowly and come to a focus way behind the lens.

Thus, when we speak of an object as being 'out of focus', we mean that it is not in focus *in the film plane* but somewhere behind or in front of it. Clearly, if the film plane can be moved back from its fixed position close to the lens, the photographer has the freedom to focus on near or distant objects just as he likes. This adjustment is usually made in practice by rotating a ring at the front of the lens assembly, the movement being transferred to the lens itself by an internal screw thread.

This system is very quick and easy to use, but there is one point to remember: it effectively moves the lens forward or back on the optical axis between subject and film plane, rather than moving the film plane in

Above left: perfectly good photographs can be taken with any camera if the subject is reasonably distant and there is good daylight. But for a wider range of possibilities—e.g. for photography in dimly lit interiors (below) or subjects requiring a 'time' exposure (above right)—an adjustable camera is needed; the 35mm SLR is the most versatile of all.

relation to the lens; this causes the image at the film plane to increase or decrease in size by a small but noticeable degree which may alter the framing of close-up shots, particularly if a tripod is in use. Therefore careful attention must be paid to this aspect of picture composition.

As an example of the adjustments that may be made, the closest focusing distance of the SMC Pentax-M f/1.7 50mm lens is 45cm (just under 18in). With suitable accessories this can be further reduced by a considerable amount (see page 141).

Technically-minded readers and those with some experience of photography may be aware that this account of focusing lenses leaves certain questions unanswered, relating in particular to the depth of the area in focus (called 'depth of field'). This we shall return to, but it will be more informative to do so by a roundabout route, taking in the subject of lens aperture on the way. But first, the problem of exposure and changing light must come under scrutiny.

Shutter speed

Of all the shortcomings of the primitive box-camera, perhaps the most inhibiting is its dependence on good daylight. When this begins to fade, whether through bad weather or the lateness of the hour, or simply because the intended subject is indoors, the camera cannot deliver a good photograph.

The original reason for having variable shutter speeds was to allow longer exposures to be made in low light, but some beautiful effects can be obtained if moving objects are photographed with a slow shutter speed. The photograph on the left was taken at 1/1000 sec, that on the right at 2 secs. The longer exposure makes a more interesting picture.

The solution is quite simple: increase either the time for which light is allowed to fall on to the film, or increase the volume of light by enlarging the aperture through which it enters the camera body. And when light deteriorates even further, both of these solutions can be employed together.

The effect of light on the silver halides in the film emulsion is cumulative, so weak light can convert them in the same pattern as strong light, although it takes longer. The emulsions used by early photographers were remarkable for their time, but grossly insensitive by today's standards. At exposure times of up to a minute or so (quite common in those days) fine timing was unnecessary as a few seconds more or less than the calculated exposure made no appreciable difference to the finished print. No mechanical shutter was needed because the photographer could start the exposure simply by uncovering the lens, and terminate it by replacing the cover.

As more sensitive emulsions were developed it became necessary to introduce a mechanically controlled shutter into camera design because the margin of tolerance (called 'exposure latitude') was very much reduced, and the human arm is too crude a mechanism to regulate movements within fractions of a second. Shutters were designed that offered variable exposure times in a series of fixed steps, and the following scale was eventually adopted as standard: 1 second, 1/2, 1/4, 1/8, 1/15, 1/30, 1/60 1/125, 1/250, 1/500, 1/1000 and 1/2000th second. Depending on design, the shutter did not necessarily offer all of these speeds. This scale is important because it is still brought into use when an automatic camera such as the ME Super is set in its manual mode. Its essential feature is that with only a slight allowance for rounding off the figures, each step exactly halves the time of the one preceding it and doubles the time of the one following it.

The focal plane shutter

There are different types of shutter mechanism but single-lens reflex cameras are usually built around what is known as a focal plane shutter. This is the only type used in current Pentax models, with the sole exception of the 110 SLR. The focal plane shutter operates across the face of the film and is structurally independent of the lens. The advantages of this design are that the lens can be freely removed even when there is a film in the camera, and that there is room in front of the shutter blinds for a mirror which reflects the light from the lens into the viewfinder (upon which the single-lens reflex principle is founded).

The mechanism of the focal plane shutter consists of a pair of opaque blinds which run vertically (as in the ME Super) or horizontally across the film gate, the interval between them being the adjustable factor. Up to a certain speed – 1/125 sec in the ME Super – the first blind completes its run before the second blind begins, so that there is a moment in time at which the film gate is completely open. Below 1/125 sec this moment becomes progressively longer. At higher speeds the second blind begins to close *before* the first has completed its run. At fast shutter speeds the gap is just a narrow slit that travels down or across the face of the film. Although this means that exposure takes place serially rather than instantaneously, the entire cycle is so rapid that even fast-moving subjects are frozen and do not discernibly 'lean' backwards on account of one end being exposed fractionally after the other.

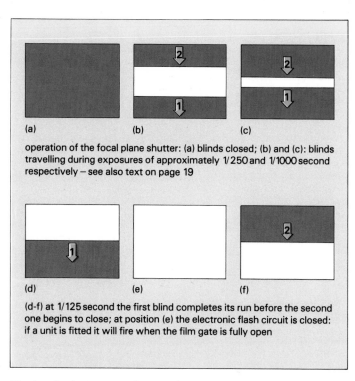

operation of the focal plane shutter: (a) blinds closed; (b) and (c): blinds travelling during exposures of approximately 1/250 and 1/1000 second respectively – see also text on page 19

(d-f) at 1/125 second the first blind completes its run before the second one begins to close; at position (e) the electronic flash circuit is closed: if a unit is fitted it will fire when the film gate is fully open

Electronic shutter speed control

The abbreviation 'electronic shutter' is often encountered, but this is slightly misleading. The electronically *controlled* shutter is spring-tensioned in the same way as its mechanical equivalent, the spring being cocked at the same time as the film is advanced. It is the delay between the activation of the two blinds, and hence the effective shutter speed, that is electronically controlled.

Shutter speed may still be selected manually if the camera design offers this facility, as it does in the case of the ME Super (see page 72); but the great benefit of the electronic timing is that an exposure meter can be incorporated into the shutter circuitry so as to adjust the shutter speed automatically according to the intensity of the light transmitted by the lens. This is *much* faster than setting the shutter speed manually in accordance with a meter read-out. Moreover, with automatic speed selection the range is stepless, whereas manually selected speeds are confined to those on the scale given on page 19. Freed from this rigid structure, the automatic system will make an exposure of the ideal duration, whether or not this is on the scale. Thus it may set a speed of, say, 1/775 sec instead of having to choose between 1/500 and 1/1000 sec.

The electronic shutter speed selection of the ME Super is fully automatic throughout the range from 4 secs to 1/2000 sec.

Lens and aperture

In terms of image sharpness the old pinhole camera was a reasonably satisfactory device. Its main inadequacy lay in the tiny volume of light admitted through the pinhole itself; this necessitated shutter speeds that would be inordinately long even with today's fast-reacting emulsions. One obvious way to solve this problem was to make the pinhole bigger: to double its area would be to halve exposure time; double it again and exposure time would be reduced to a quarter of the original, and so on. The diagram shows why this does not work: a pinhole permits only a thin, thread-like beam of light from any single point to pass through it; other rays from the same point are masked off, and the resulting image is fairly sharp. A wider opening lets through cone-like bundles of light rays, so that any single point on the subject is represented in the image by a featureless disc of light, and no clear image of the object is formed.

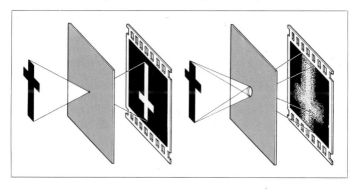

A tiny pinhole masks off most of the light rays reflected from a single point, enabling fine lines to be etched on the film. A larger opening does not mask selectively enough.

The logical step is to add a convex lens, a simple example of which has already been described (page 15).

Modern adjustable lenses have within them an assembly of interleaved metal plates forming a roughly circular opening. These plates are linked to a ring on the lens housing. Rotating the ring causes the plates to pivot inwards or outwards, altering the diameter of the aperture and regulating thereby the volume of light passing through the lens.

Given the extreme sensitivity of most photographic emulsions, precise control over lens aperture is vital, just as it is with shutter speed. Therefore, each time the area of the aperture (*not* its diameter) is doubled or halved the setting ring comes to a click-stop—a slight but definite resistance which marks precise points on a continuously variable scale. For ultra-fine control, there is usually a click-stop at the intermediate stage half-way between the numbered settings as well, but this may not be the case. The photographer must be aware of the position of the click-stops with any lens he is using, because the aperture if often set by touch alone. The following calibrations are engraved on the aperture setting ring: 22, 16, 11,

8, 5.6, 4, 2.8, 2, 1.4. The interval between any two of these is known as a 'stop' or 'f/stop', a term which in common use is often extended to include the step between adjacent settings on the shutter speed scale.

The derivation of the numerical values on the above scale is explained elsewhere (see page 123); for the moment it is adequate to note that a high number denotes a small aperture, and a low number a large one.

Variations may occur at either extreme of the scale. In particular, the largest available aperture may be between two values, so that a figure of, say, 1.7 may conclude the scale.

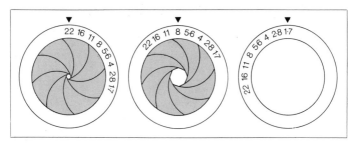

Above: high f/numbers denote small apertures and low numbers wide apertures. If you want to watch this happening with your Pentax lens, first remove it from the camera (taking great care not to touch the glass elements) and turn the aperture ring.

Below: in situations like this you would normally use the widest aperture your lens can offer.

Reciprocity

Variable shutter speeds and lens apertures provide two methods of adjusting a camera to cater for fluctuations in the intensity of light. Although numerically very different the two scales have one vital link: the step from one calibration to the next alters the exposure by the same factor. Increasing the exposure by one stop on either scale *doubles* the amount of light passing through the lens, while it follows that reducing the exposure by one stop *halves* the amount.

This means that in average lighting conditions there is a choice of f/stop-shutter speed combinations which all yield the same result, at least in terms of the quantity of light transmitted. If for any reason it is considered desirable to adjust either lens aperture or shutter speed once a correct combination has been established (and there can be many reasons for this) then the other *must be reciprocally altered by the same number of stops* in order to restore the exposure to the original correct value.

This is of course only possible within the physical limitations of the two mechanisms in use. In extreme lighting conditions the number of combinations available becomes progressively less.

The reciprocity law can be safely applied except when shutter speed is faster than 1/1000 second or slower than about 1 second. Outside these extremes photographic emulsions lose their capacity to react at a constant and predictable rate. This is especially important with colour emulsions, the three layers of which react at different rates even on the same film: this can result in a pronounced colour cast over images made at excessively slow or fast shutter speeds. The effect is known as 'reciprocity failure'.

Exposure settings – lens aperture and shutter speed – must work *together* to balance the amount of light available, taking into account the sensitivity (ASA rating) of the film.

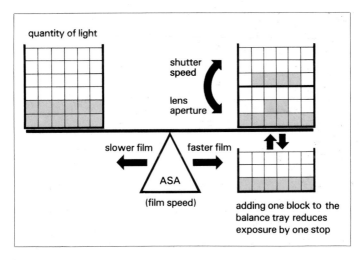

quantity of light

shutter speed

lens aperture

slower film   faster film

ASA

(film speed)

adding one block to the balance tray reduces exposure by one stop

Exposure metering

The idea sometimes expounded that light levels can be assessed by eye alone is false. The eye adapts very easily to a very wide range of light levels and it is only when major and abrupt changes take place that we are made aware of it. At best an approximation can be achieved by taking stock of known phenomena from which the intensity of the prevailing light can be deduced: the presence or absence of hard shadows cast by the sun, or the nature and thickness of cloud in the sky, are useful pointers. This is the basis of the tables supplied by film manufacturers to assist photographers who do not have the use of a meter.

For consistent success, however, a light meter is indispensable, and nowadays all but the most basic cameras have such a meter built into them.

The main component of an exposure meter is a light-sensitive cell. In the past selenium cell and then cadmium sulphide (CdS) cell meters were common, but although meters of either type may be encountered in many cameras still in use, both are obsolescent in new camera design due to the development of more efficient types. Silicon photo diodes (or SPDs) react faster than the older cells and have achieved widespread acceptance among manufacturers. However, there is an even newer light sensor now available—the gallium arsenide phosphide photo diode (GaAsP-PD, or GPD), which is unique to Pentax and which is used in the ME Super, ME-F and the MX.

Formerly, an exposure meter was an optional extra, separate from the camera. Lens aperture and shutter speed were read off from a dial which was set according to film speed and an 'exposure value' indicated by the meter needle. After a while smaller meters were developed, and it became feasible to build them into the camera body itself and couple them to the lens aperture and shutter speed controls. However, it was an innovation of major importance when the Asahi Optical Co devised the first through-the-lens (TTL) metering system and used it in the Pentax Spotmatic; this system was subsequently adopted as standard by all leading camera manufacturers. The obvious benefit of through-the-lens metering is that the light measured is *only* that used to make the picture: stray light from other sources cannot interfere with the reading.

In practice it has proved possible to refine this system further still. As not all subjects are illuminated over the entire image area it is logical to restrict the metering to the most important part of the subject. If the *entire* area is metered, a brilliantly lit background (such as the sky) can influence the meter to underexpose the subject, while a dark background can have precisely the opposite effect. Only the photographer can decide which is the most important part of the scene before him, so a degree of compromise is inevitable with any system which seeks to concentrate on one part of the image at the expense of others. However, experience has shown that the most generally useful form of selectivity is that offered by a *centre-weighted* reading, i.e. one in which a relatively small area in the centre makes the dominant contribution to the total reading, with progressively less importance being attached to localized bright spots or shadows as the edges of the frame are approached (see diagram). This will result in a higher proportion of correctly exposed pictures than any other system with uncritical acceptance by the photographer, but it is not—nor is it intended

The light meter of the ME Super is of the centre-weighted type, which means that it is more sensitive to light coming from the middle of the subject than from the background. This is ideal for the majority of photographs.

to be—a substitute for the intelligence of the mind behind the camera. You should learn to recognize situations in which the meter reading is inappropriate for the subject and compensate accordingly (see pages 68-71 and 73-75).

Shutter speed and subject movement

Though usually short in duration, exposure takes place over a finite period, i.e. it has a beginning and an end. If a subject or part of a subject moves during that period its outline and surface detail will be confused in the photographic image. If it is displaced by more than its own area it will often appear transparent and very probably unidentifiable for what it is. In exposures lasting several seconds or more, moving objects may, depending on their speed, pass right through the frame without leaving any detectable trace at all.

This peculiarly photographic phenomenon is examined in detail later. However, there is one point worth making here: if a camera is not held quite steady when the shutter is released it will record movement, known as 'camera shake', over the entire image (sometimes more on one side than the other if the shutter has been stabbed at instead of gently released). The slower the shutter speed in use, the greater the risk of this marring the photograph. The best policy is to avoid using shutter speeds of less than 1/60 sec if at all possible. Most people can probably get away with 1/30 sec. But at slower speeds, if it is not possible to bring them back within the 'safe' range by selecting a wider aperture, the camera really needs to be mounted on a tripod or similar support.

Depth of field

This is where the threads left hanging loose at the end of the section on focusing lenses (page 18) are drawn together again.

Whatever point a lens is focused on, image sharpness always extends some distance in front of that point (i.e. towards the camera) and a greater distance behind it. The distance from the nearest to the furthest points of sharp focus is called 'depth of field'. This sharpness is in fact an illusion, created by the fact that as actual focus is approached the degree of softness (the 'spread' of an image point that is not absolutely in focus) dwindles beyond the level at which the human eye—fallible as it is—can tell whether focus is reached or not. The largest disc that the eye accepts as a literal point is known as the 'circle of confusion'. This is, so to speak, the half-penny coin of the visual currency: it is indivisible even though the value of objects may be less than the sum it represents. If the eye were optically perfect and the photographic image consisted of continuous tone instead of a pattern of black grains, then sharpness would be observed to be confined to a flat plane at the exact distance on which the lens was focused.

This is of interest, but of no great importance to the photographer planning his shot. It is more valuable to look at the factors that govern depth of field in practice. These are (i) lens aperture, (ii) focusing distance

Restricting depth of field makes a subject stand out sharply against a background that might otherwise be distracting.

and (iii) focal length of lens. Of these, only the first two factors are relevant here. The effects of focal length are described on page 126.

Depth of field is at its greatest with small apertures and at its shallowest with large apertures.

Depth of field is at its greatest when the lens is focused on a distant point and at its shallowest at close focusing distances.

When these factors are working together they compound each other and the effects are very marked indeed.

To work out the depth of field that will result from any given combination of aperture and focusing distance is simple enough after a little practice. Both the focusing distance and the f/number in use are aligned with the same fixed mark on the top of the lens housing. On either side of this mark the f/number scale is repeated, with the lower number inmost (there is not always a calibration for every f/number, and some calibrations may be left unlabelled for lack of space). The two numbers on the fixed scale that correspond to the f/number in use will indicate on the focusing ring the nearest (to the right in Pentax SMC lenses) and furthest (to the left) limits of sharp focus.

Any precise statement of depth of field, whether presented as a scale, a table, a graph, a diagram or anything else, is so literal that it carries the risk of masking an important optical fact: that sharpness falls off at a variable rate. The following is a useful rule of thumb: if depth of field is extensive, objects well outside the limits of sharp focus may be only *slightly* out of focus; if depth of field is shallow, even objects *only just* outside the limits will probably be indecipherably blurred.

In some pictures the zone of interest may extend for miles, so maximum depth of field is essential.

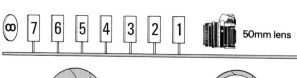

50mm lens

 f/22   f/2

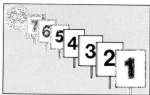

lens focused at 2m
depth of field 1.2-4.5m

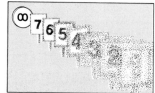

lens focused at 2m
depth of field 1.9-2.1m

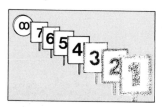

lens focused at ∞
depth of field 3.4m- ∞

lens focused at ∞
depth of field 37m- ∞

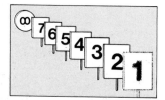

lens focused at 5m
depth of field 2m- ∞

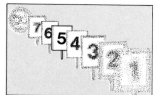

lens focused at 5m
depth of field 4.4-5.7m

Lens aperture and focusing distance both affect depth of field: study
the diagrams carefully to see how this works. In particular, compare
the extremes represented by the diagrams at top right and bottom left.

3 The 35mm single-lens reflex camera

The aspects of photography discussed so far in this book apply equally to all adjustable cameras. However, there is one design that for quality combined with versatility stands on its own: the 35mm single-lens reflex.

The 35mm film format

Film can be commercially obtained in sheets and in rolls of various sizes. A large film area gives excellent definition because grain is small relative to total image size, but large-format cameras are bulky and not usually very mobile.

At the other end of the scale a film format such as 110, with an image area that measures 13 × 17mm, fits into tiny cameras that can be slipped into the pocket; however, image quality is good only as long as grain does not become obtrusive, which it can do at higher magnifications.

For the majority of photographers the 35mm (or 135) film format represents the ideal compromise. Image area is 24 × 36mm, which is large enough to yield prints in which grain is not evident even when enlarged to exhibition sizes. At the same time the 35mm film cassette is small and can be easy to load (depending on the care taken by camera manufacturers in designing a loading system), so that the standard hardware—camera body and lens—need not be bulky or unmanageable.

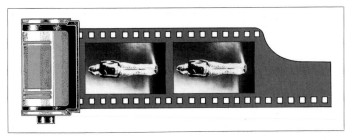

35mm film is usually purchased in cassettes like that illustrated above, the most popular films being available in 12, 24 or 36 exposure rolls. Though small and easy to handle, 35mm negatives can be extensively cropped and still give acceptable prints — the one on the right was made from about one-sixth of the negative area.

Reflex viewing

A *reflex* camera is one in which the image viewed is a mirror *reflection* rather than direct vision of the world before the lens. The mirror of a *single-lens* reflex camera is situated at an angle of 45° to the lens axis, and reflects the light entering the lens upwards on to a ground-glass screen which is set horizontally in the roof of the camera body. The distance between lens and screen via the mirror is exactly the same as between lens and film, so that the image formed on the screen is identical to that which will be formed on the film when the mirror is removed.

The single-lens reflex (SLR) camera body is surmounted by a characteristic hump, somewhat like a pyramid in shape, which houses a five-sided prism or 'pentaprism'. Introduced by the Asahi Optical Company of Tokyo in 1957, this design breakthrough has proved to be of fundamental importance to the course of modern photography; the name Pentax is in fact derived from the word pentaprism.

Before this development, eye-level reflex viewing had not been practical: to divert the image formed by the lens upwards by means of conventional mirrors in a periscope arrangement would have resulted in lateral reversal of the image in the viewfinder. Some people might have been prepared to get used to this when framing static subjects in a horizontal format, but the difficulties of following a moving subject and of coping with inverted viewing presented much greater difficulties. The pentaprism corrects the image so that what the photographer sees is both the right way up and the right way round.

With viewing problems solved, the advantages of using the same lens for both viewing and exposure are immense. Accurate framing becomes possible with lenses of any focal length and at any camera-to-subject distance. It is not practical to use a wide range of lenses — especially zoom lenses — with camera in which the viewfinding and picture-taking systems are separate; nor are such cameras very well adapted for close-up photography on account of the discrepancies in framing that arise when the viewfinder is displaced from the lens-subject axis. Ideally, every lens should have its own viewfinder — which is effectively what single-lens reflex viewing offers, even when highly specialized scientific instruments such as microscopes or telescopes are fitted in place of regular photographic lenses.

A lens 'sees' things upside-down and back-to-front, and this made reflex photography of moving subjects very difficult before the pentaprism was developed.

The interchangeability of parts

Being modular in concept, 35mm SLR systems are economical as well as versatile. The far-sighted first-time camera buyer can start with an inexpensive body and a standard lens, and need never buy anything more except a supply of film. But if, as it often happens, the habit of photography takes root and the camera owner's enthusiasm grows as he becomes accustomed to the act of photographing and the unabating pleasure of seeing newly processed films for the first time—then the possibilities are almost inexhaustible. One or more lenses can be added as and when the money becomes available, followed perhaps by a set of filters or some close-up equipment; and if one day it is decided that the original body is no longer adequate to meet the photographer's increased demands and must be exchanged for one that has more facilities, the lenses and accessories need not be discarded or sold off cheaply: they simply become part of a new system. Selective upgrading is always possible, provided that the first camera and lens are chosen from a broad and reliable range.

Other manufacturers, notably lens makers, wisely take steps to ensure that their products are compatible with the Pentax K bayonet mounting system. However, these are not necessarily engineered and produced to the precise standards which Pentax meticulously apply to their own lenses and accessories. The very best choice is *always* to buy a lens which is made by the manufacturer of the body it is to be used with. Pentax

This monstrous wide-angle view was taken with a lens of 20mm focal length — very easy to do with an SLR.

In a matter of seconds a standard lens can be changed for a special close-up or 'macro' lens.

camera bodies and the SMC range of lenses are conceived as parts of a total system and are designed to work together for optimum image quality. However, where cost is the overriding consideration it can sometimes be an acceptable compromise to choose one of the less expensive lenses now available in large numbers, but your attention is drawn to the following statement which forms part of the standard Pentax guarantee: *'Because the tolerances, quality, and design compatibility of lenses other than Pentax lenses are beyond our control, damage caused by use of such lenses will not be covered by this warranty policy.'*

SLR mechanisms

Loading and film advance in 35mm SLR cameras is a procedure that does not vary much from one range to the next, the main difference being in the design of the take-up spool. The exceptionally easy process of loading the ME Super and other Pentax cameras is described on page 51.

Focusing

Since in SLR photography the user is looking at an image formed on a screen by the picture-taking lens when he frames his shot, it is an easy matter to check visually whether the subject is in focus. However, focusing is more difficult in some situations than in others, and is always more critical with wide apertures than with narrow ones. The screens are therefore equipped with focusing aids, the most generally useful of which is the split-image rangefinder. In this system a circle in the centre of the screen is divided (usually horizontally) into two halves. Any straight line that passes through the central circle will appear broken, the fragments being progressively less displaced as exact focusing is approached (see the illustrations below). Another, not dissimilar, system consists of a central microprism grid which breaks the image up into a pattern of tiny fragments. Until the image is in exact focus these appear to flicker with the inevitable slight movements of the hands. The screen fitted to the ME Super combines both systems, having a central split-image spot surrounded by a microprism collar, thereby giving the best of both worlds.

The exposure

When the shutter is released the following train of events is initiated, the basics of which are common to all SLR cameras: (i) the iris diaphragm closes to its preselected setting; (ii) the hinged mirror swings up out of the

How a split image rangefinder works in a single-lens reflex camera: any object that is not in focus appears distinctly broken until exact focusing is established.

light path; (iii) the shutter opens and closes; (iv) the mirror returns to its original position, and (v) the iris diaphragm returns to full aperture.

Steps (i) and (ii) are in fact simultaneous, as are steps (iv) and (v), so that all the photographer experiences is a momentary loss of vision in the viewfinder while the mirror is in the raised position.

Film advance

Once the shutter has been released the spring must be retensioned before the next exposure can be made. This retensioning or 'cocking' of the shutter is performed with the same lever—situated to the right, where the photographer's thumb rests, in standard design—as is used to advance the film. Combining the two functions in the same action not only makes for speed of operation; it has the added advantage that an exposed frame cannot be accidentally double-exposed, nor can a blank frame be wound on until it has been exposed.

In SLRs film is advanced on the 'one-stroke' principle, i.e. turning the lever until a dead stop is felt advances the film by exactly the right amount (8 sprocket perforations per frame).

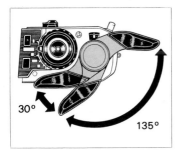

The film advance lever of the ME Super: a 30° standoff angle makes it possible to leave the thumb hooked in for quick sequences of exposures; the 135° throw brings an unexposed frame to the film gate in a single stroke.

Open-aperture metering

Things were not always so easy for the user of the SLR camera. At one time the iris diaphragm had to be stopped down manually after framing of the shot and before exposure, and this was naturally a serious obstacle to action photography. Furthermore the mirror stayed in its exposure position until the film was advanced, so that total image black-out followed every shot. The instant-return mirror, a milestone in SLR camera design, was first introduced by Pentax.

The mechanical stopping down of the diaphragm as part of the shutter releasing cycle—often referred to as 'automatic' but not to be confused with any system of automatic exposure control—not only enabled the photographer to view his subject unhampered right up until the moment of exposure: it also opened the way for what is known as *open aperture metering*. In this system it is the aperture control ring only, and not the iris diaphragm itself, that is coupled to the exposure meter. This is far more convenient in use than *stop-down metering*, in which the diaphragm must be closed down to the set aperture so that the meter can indicate whether the light transmitted by the lens is of the correct intensity. When the lens is stopped down to small apertures the viewfinder can become so dark that the meter needle cannot be seen.

4 SLR features and facilities

Listed below are the most important features and facilities available on modern SLR cameras, together with brief descriptions of how they work and situations in which they are useful. In some cases cross-references are given to fuller descriptions elsewhere in this book.

The main purpose of this section is to elucidate SLR jargon for the benefit of those not well versed in it; it is hoped that it will also provide a useful reference section for more experienced photographers and help the prospective buyer to narrow down the choice to a model which most exactly balances his needs with his means. To this end, each description begins with a list of current 35mm Pentax models bearing the feature described. All descriptions refer to Pentax models and cannot necessarily be applied to cameras from other ranges even where terminology is similar.

Automatic exposure control (LX, ME Super, ME-F, MG) Exposure control may be *fully automatic*, so that the user sets neither lens aperture nor shutter speed; this system is employed in the Pentax Auto 110, but rejected in all 35mm models as it deprives the photographer of the means of exercising true creative control. Systems requiring the user to set either the aperture or the shutter speed, known as *aperture priority* or *shutter priority* respectively, are almost always preferred by serious amateur and professional photographers. Pentax automatic SLRs all employ the aperture priority system: as the aperture setting ring is almost adjacent to the focusing ring on the majority of lenses it is possible to react instantly to fluid situations and unpredictable lighting, without even removing the camera from the eye.

There are still photographers who are suspicious of any form of automation. This is quite unnecessary: the aperture priority system merely performs with unparalleled accuracy and speed a function which the photographer would otherwise have to waste his own time on. Shutter speed can be altered very simply by resetting the aperture—which would have to be done anyway. Provided that the camera offers an exposure compensation facility and manual override (see below) it is no less of a creative tool than any equivalent manual camera.

Exposure compensation (LX, ME Super, ME-F, MG) There are certain lighting conditions, notably where strong backlighting or high contrast prevails, in which the reading given by a TTL exposure meter is known not to provide the best results. With experience these conditions can be quickly recognized by the photographer. The exposure compensation dial enables him to increase or decrease the exposure by one or two stops—enough to handle most situations—while retaining all the benefits of automatic exposure control. In aperture priority systems it is the shutter speed that is altered; the compensated speed, not the original speed, is indicated in the viewfinder (ME Super and LX) together with a warning that an exposure factor is in use: this ensures that a factor is not set for one exposure and then forgotten, to the detriment of the rest of the film. The exposure factors are as follows:

$4\times$ = 2 stops over	$\frac{1}{2}\times$ = 1 stop under
$2\times$ = 1 stop over	$\frac{1}{4}\times$ = 2 stops under
$1\times$ = normal as metered	

Manual override (LX, ME Super, ME-F) It is not desirable to use automatic exposure in all circumstances, even with the compensation facility. Sophisticated automatics are therefore equipped with a means of disconnecting the light meter from the electronic shutter circuitry and reverting to full manual operation. Chapter 8, *The ME Super on manual*, is entirely devoted to this subject. Note, however, that when the ME Super, ME-F and LX are used in their manual modes, the TTL meter can still be used independently; also, shutter speed control is still electronic.

Stepless electronic shutter control (LX, ME Super, ME-F, MG) Electronic control of shutter mechanisms refers only to the *timing* of the exposure. The power required to activate the shutter is provided mechanically by a spring, which is tensioned by the film advance lever. Control is *stepless* when speed selection is continuous throughout the range, i.e. not pegged to a scale. (See pages 19-20)

B setting (LX, ME Super, ME-F, MG, K1000, MX) When the exposure mode dial or shutter speed dial is set to 'B' (Bulb) the shutter remains open for as long as the release button is kept depressed, making possible time exposures lasting from a few seconds—e.g. for photographing fireworks, to several hours—e.g. in astrophotography. 'B' is always a manual setting.

An example of when the B setting is needed: you never know how long it may be necessary to wait for lightning to strike within the picture area. If your cable release has a locking screw you will not need to hold the shutter release down.

Shutter cocked indicator (LX, ME Super, ME-F, MG, K1000, MX) Provides quick visual means of checking whether or not the camera is ready to shoot; saves fumbling with the film advance lever.

Exposure lock (ME Super, ME-F, LX, MX) Prevents accidental shutter release, e.g. in transit; also prevents meter being unintentionally being switched on and hence conserves battery life.

Self-timer (LX, ME Super, ME-F, MG, MX) Also called 'delayed action shutter release', the self-timer is a clockwork mechanism for delaying the exposure by a variable period of up to about 12 seconds.

Random access multiple exposure facility (LX) Double or multiple exposures are possible with all Pentax 35mm SLRs although not with random access. With the random access feature of the LX multiple exposures can be made on any frame in the roll as long as the film has not been disengaged from the teeth on the sprocket wheel.

Exposure counter (LX, ME Super, ME-F, MG, K1000, MX) Keeps a running total of the number of frames exposed; is automatically reset to zero each time the back is opened.

Depth of field preview (LX, MX) Stops down the iris diaphragm enabling depth of field to be checked visually through the viewfinder; complements the depth of field scale marked on most lenses, showing not only actual depth of field, but also the rate at which focus falls off.

Mirror lock (LX) Facility for locking the mirror in its 'up' position out of the light path; minimizes the effects of vibration caused by the action of the mirror—negligible in normal photography but sometimes discernible in certain types of macro work and photomicrography.

Magic needle loading (LX, ME Super, ME-F, MG, MX) A real innovation in an area of camera design that is curiously neglected by some manufacturers, the magic needle system enables the film leader to be inserted at any angle between any two of sixteen rods or 'needles' on the take-up spool; winding on the film until the perforations are engaged on the sprocket wheel automatically corrects the angle and takes up any slack.

Memo holder (LX, ME Super, ME-F, MX) Frame on the standard camera back designed to hold the top of a film box, so that information about film type, number of exposures on the roll, speed and so on is permanently available. This is invaluable for people who change film types often.

Film transport indicator (ME Super, ME-F) A small window in the back of the top plate beneath the film advance lever, in which red and black stripes oscillate when a correctly loaded film is being advanced or rewound.

Batteryless operation (LX, ME Super, ME-F, MG) All Pentax SLR cameras with electronically controlled shutters have at least one failsafe mechanical shutter speed. For convenience, this is the same speed at which the shutter is synchronized for flash, which means that the user needs only to leave the mode selector in the 'X' position for the mechanical speed to be permanently engaged. The LX offers a much greater range of mechanical shutter speeds; see page 39.

Interchangeable lenses (LX, ME Super, ME-F, MG, K1000, MX) All current Pentax 35mm SLR camera bodies are equipped with the Pentax K bayonet mounting system, ensuring total compatibility between Pentax SMC lenses and bodies.

 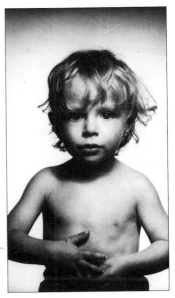

The self-timer enables you to take a photograph of yourself,
as well as having other uses – this child's attention was firmly
held by the whirring noise, which helped to overcome the
problem of getting him to look at the camera and stay still.

Interchangeable viewfinders (LX) Although the standard viewfinder is
adequate for most people in most situations, interchangeable viewfinders
represent a great refinement for people with poor eyesight, for certain
specialized applications, and for people who prefer waist-level viewing.
See page 40.

Interchangeable focusing screens (LX, MX) These make hairpin
accuracy possible when focusing lenses of extreme focal lengths;
especially useful in scientific work.

Interchangeable data back (LX, ME Super, ME-F, MG, MX) Can be
fitted in place of the standard back; converts the SLR into a data camera
which can record date and time, exposure settings or other information on
to each frame. Especially useful for scientific work.

Through-the-lens exposure metering (LX, ME Super, ME-F, MG,
K1000, MX) System of measuring only the light that enters the lens,
ensuring an unprecedented degree of accuracy combined with convenience. See page 24.

Centre-weighted metering (LX, ME Super, ME-F, MG, MX) The
system of TTL light measurement which gives the most consistently good
results is that which responds with increasing sensitivity towards the
centre of the image area, the peripheral areas being largely ignored. See
page 25.

Automatic meter shut-off (LX, ME Super, ME-F, MG, MX) In order to conserve battery life the exposure meter, which is activated in the Pentax models listed by slight pressure on the shutter release button, is automatically cut out after about 30 seconds. If an exposure is made or if the meter is reactivated by a further touch on the button, the display is instantly re-illuminated.

Integrated direct metering (LX) Used with automatic exposure control, IDM light measurement is based on light reflected from the film plane during the actual exposure—either from the surface of the emulsion itself or from a fixed pattern on the first shutter blind: the former in the case of slow to medium speeds and the latter in the case of high speeds. Thus, rapid changes in light level are accommodated as the exposure is being made; with conventional systems the meter is 'blinded' for the duration of the exposure.

Hot shoe (LX, ME Super, ME-F, MG, K1000, MX) Accessory shoe on top of the camera with a contact terminal for cordless synchronization of electronic flash with the shutter mechanism.

X-synch socket (LX, ME Super, ME-F, K1000, MX) Socket for connection of electronic flash units equipped with a cord. When the mode selection dial or shutter speed dial is set to 'X' the circuit is closed to synchronize the flash with the full open position of the shutter. The shutter speed at which this takes place varies between cameras.

Through-the-lens flash metering (LX) Provision for dedicated flash units to be controlled by the IDM system described above rather than by the sensor built into the unit itself. The advantages of this are that any aperture can be used, so simplifying flash procedure; that flash used as fill-in lighting with daylight shots will be metered together with the ambient light; that flash bounced from various surfaces and/or used with filters over the camera lens will be correctly metered at the film plane, and that flash units set off by other photographers will be metered and taken into account.

Dedicated flash facility (LX, ME Super, ME-F, MG) When a dedicated Pentax flash unit is fitted to the hot shoe the camera automatically moves into the electronic flash mode, and essential information about synchronization and capacitor charge, which normally must be read from the unit itself, is relayed into the viewfinder. See also chapter 10.

Motor winder facility (LX, ME Super, ME-F, MG, MX) Sometimes also called an 'autowinder', the motor winder can be attached to the tripod socket on the base plate of the camera. It can be set either to advance the film automatically after each exposure to make fast but controlled sequences of shots possible, or to make consecutive exposures at a rate of about 1.5-2 frames per second (shutter speed permitting). Either way, exposures are individually metered when the motor winder is used with a camera set in its automatic mode.

Motor drive facility (LX, MX) The motor drive advances and exposes film at a variable rate of up to 5 frames per second, shutter speed permitting. The unit is the basis of a system of accessories that includes a bulk film back to hold a 250-frame length of film, a battery grip, a battery pack, an AC power pack and other accessories. It can also be used for single frame advance and to rewind film rapidly into its cassette.

5 The Pentax range of cameras

Pentax LX

Aperture-priority automatic 35mm SLR with full manual override, IDM metering, TTL flash metering, interchangeable viewfinders and many more features. This is a professional SLR system incorporating the best of everything, for the photographer who cannot afford not to have the most versatile system that money can buy. Space does not permit a complete breakdown of the facilities offered by the LX, but the following are some of the more important ones. See also the chart on page 48.

IDM light measurement

Conventional automatic exposure systems are 'blinded' at the moment of exposure, so that alterations in light levels that occur after the shutter has opened (e.g. car lights appearing or disappearing, or other photographers using flash) result in incorrect exposure. With integrated direct metering the new-generation SPD calculates the light as it is reflected from the film plane—from the emulsion itself or from a pattern on the first shutter blind—

during exposure, and reacts almost instantaneously to sudden fluctuations in the intensity of the light transmitted by the lens. Among other things this also makes TTL flash metering possible, at any aperture, and two powerful new flash units are available which have been designed to exploit this facility to the full—the AF 280T and the AF 400T (see page 117).

Failsafe manual speeds
The normal electronically controlled range of manual speeds is from 1/2000 down to 4 secs. If batteries fail or expire, six manual speeds from 1/2000 sec to X can be selected. No other SLR has this capability.

Interchangeable viewfinders
The unique system of interchangeable viewfinders is designed to extend the use of the LX into the remotest corners of technical, industrial and scientific photography as well as to facilitate its use in 'normal' difficult circumstances. The FB-1 System Finder is especially versatile, as it has three interchangeable eyepieces—Standard Eyepiece, Action Eyepiece and Magni-Eyepiece—making what amounts to a system within a system. This represents a genuine advance in SLR design.

Random access multiple exposure
A feature for the adventurous photographer who likes to manipulate and interpret as well as record. Any previously exposed frame on a roll of film can be located provided the film has not been wound off the take-up spool. When second or subsequent exposures have been completed the film is returned to the unexposed length within a tolerance of 0.2mm.

The full information viewfinder of the LX. The aperture selected is displayed at the top through an oblique-reading prism that looks out on to the actual setting ring; shutter speed and exposure meter information are shown on the right. A red flag (top right) indicates that an exposure factor is in use, while a blue flag indicates shutter speed when the camera is in its manual mode.

Pentax ME-F

Aperture-priority automatic 35mm SLR with full electro-mechanical manual override, fully automatic focusing when used with the SMC Pentax AF Zoom 35-70mm f/2.8, and electronic focusing guidance with most SMC Pentax lenses.

The auto focus system is of the contrast type, which is a passive system controlled from within the camera body. Unlike active systems, which establish subject distance by sending out signals, and which are misled by transparent surfaces such as window glass, the contrast system is based on photometric analysis of the image in a plane equivalent to the focal plane. Comparative readings from two rows of cells indicate the direction in which image contrast is stronger. When the same level of contrast is recorded by both rows of cells the subject is in focus.

When SMC Pentax lenses not having the auto focus facility are fitted the information from the photometric cells is relayed to an LED display in the viewfinder, where it is presented as an arrow indicating which way the focusing ring should be turned. This is done manually. When optimum focus is reached the red LED arrow is extinguished and a large green LED lights up, accompanied optionally by an audible signal.

The SMC Pentax AF Zoom 35-70mm f/2.8

This is the first of a new series of SMC Pentax auto focus lenses, each equipped with its own power system for automatic focusing at the touch of a button. The photographer activates the focusing micromotor and the contrast information from the photometric cells, instead of being relayed into the viewfinder, is transmitted electronically to the lens. When optimum focus is reached the barrel stops moving automatically and the green LED lights up accompanied by the audible signal. Although the technology is advanced the system is extremely simple to use, and unlike the conventional split image rangefinder is completely unambiguous.

Other features

The exposure meter of the ME-F is of the gallium arsenide phosphide photo diode type used in the ME Super and MX, and is linked to a viewfinder display consisting of fourteen LEDs. Exposure control is aperture-priority automatic with full manual override, incorporating the futuristic shutter-dial-less electro-manual system developed for the ME Super.

Flash synchronization and flash ready information appear automatically in the viewfinder when Pentax dedicated electronic flash units are fitted. Also, the Winder ME-II can be fitted to the ME-F for both single-frame and continuous film advance. In its single-frame mode it can be used in conjunction with the 35-70mm auto focus to provide an unprecedented degree of automation.

The special feature of the ME-F viewfinder is the LED display at the bottom which gives focusing information.When the AF Zoom 35-70mm lens is fitted, focusing is carried out electronically at the touch of a button.With other SMC Pentax lenses the photometric image analysis sytem gives absolutely clear and unambiguous information, in the form of arrows which indicate the direction in which the focusing ring must be turned. A green LED signifies spot-on focusing.

Pentax MG

Aperture-priority auto-only 35mm SLR with viewfinder LED display giving exposure information. This camera caters for the photographer who does not want full manual override, but who nevertheless wants to be aware of the automatic exposure settings. Apart from this the MG offers many of the advantages of the ME Super, and the absence of the manual override facility is reflected in the price.

The camera is exceptionally simple in use: all the photographer needs to do is focus the lens and check the colour of the LED illuminated in the viewfinder, adjusting the aperture ring only if there is a danger of incorrect exposure or camera shake. Aperture-priority automatic exposure does, however, allow the photographer considerable freedom of choice in most situations should he wish to exercise it: shutter speed can be selected indirectly for a particular effect (such as panning, or freezing fast-moving action) by adjustment of the aperture ring. This can be very quickly achieved as the focusing ring and aperture ring are conveniently close together on most lenses. There is also an exposure compensation facility of 2 stops each way; in cases where this proves inadequate further compensation can be obtained by adjustment of the ASA dial.

The LED display in the viewfinder of the MG is colour-coded so that it is almost impossible to take a bad photograph. At the same time it offers the more ambitious photographer the chance to exercise control over his exposure.

Pentax K1000

Manual only 35mm SLR with built-in zero-method TTL exposure metering. The K1000 is designed to offer Pentax quality as economically as possible; therefore extras are excluded from the design. However, no attempt has been made to economize on the essential working parts—the K1000 is a genuine Pentax, and of course the bayonet mount is the standard Pentax-K type and accepts all the SMC lenses and other accessories listed on page 130-144. The shutter speed range is generous— 1/1000 sec down to 1 sec with a B setting—and film speeds of 20 to 3200 ASA can be set.

The meter is activated by removal of the lens cap and cut out when this is replaced. The camera is synchronized for electronic flash via the hot shoe or a cord socket.

The K1000 is ideal for those who require the reliability and versatility provided by a major system manufacturer for the least outlay; also, anyone who wants a spare camera body for use in emergencies may prefer this model to one of the more sophisticated ones.

The K1000 has zero-method open-aperture exposure metering: this means that when the floating needle is exactly centred, exposure settings are correct. The plus sign indicates overexposure, the minus sign underexposure.

Pentax MX

Manual-only 35mm SLR with centre-weighted TTL exposure metering and full information viewfinder. The MX is for the photographer who needs a camera of advanced specifications but who is unwilling to accept automatic exposure control. It is professional in scope, having a system of 8 interchangeable focusing screens and facility for motor drive as well as winder. All exposure information is clearly visible in the viewfinder: an oblique-reading prism window looks out directly on to the aperture ring, while shutter speed is displayed alongside a panel of 5 LEDs indicating correct exposure and up to 1 stop over or under exposure. This makes total manual control as easy as it can be, but the camera never threatens to take over the photographer's role.

Shutter speed range is from 1/1000 to 1 sec plus B setting, with flash synchronization for both electronic units and bulb flashguns.

The full-information view-finder of the MX. Aperture setting can be viewed through the prism window at the top, while shutter speed is displayed on the right together with a simple LED panel showing over, under or correct exposure.

Pentax Auto 110 SLR

Fully automatic 110 SLR with TTL metering and bayonet mount accepting a range of five interchangeable lenses. The tiny Auto 110 SLR is a system camera for people who find the 35mm format bulky or unmanageable, or who want a second system with which they can travel light.

The complete system consists of the following.

Pentax Auto 110 camera body
Pentax 110 Auto Winder for single frame film-advance
Pentax 110 24mm f/2.8 standard lens
Pentax 110 18mm f/2.8 wide-angle lens
Pentax 110 50mm f/2.8 telephoto lens
Pentax 110 70mm f/2.8 telephoto lens
Pentax 110 20–40mm f/2.8 zoom lens
Lens attachments for 24mm f/2.8: close-up attachments S31 and S16; UV and skylight filters; lens hood
Lens attachments for 18mm f/2.8: close-up attachment W21; UV and skylight filters; lens hood
Lens attachments for 50mm f/2.8: close-up attachments T86 and T43; UV and skylight filters; lens hood
The 70mm telephoto and 20–40mm zoom lenses have a 49mm filter thread and thus accept the standard 35mm format attachments
Eyepiece correction lenses (− 5 − + 3 dioptres)
AF-100P and AF-130P electronic auto flash units
Strap, gadget bag, lens caps, body mount cap, tripod spacer (for 50mm lens), chain strap, soft cases.

An entire system consisting of most of the above items is available in its own carrying case.

110 film (image size 13 × 17mm) is purchased in cartridges, which are simply inserted into the back of the camera; film speed is set automatically by notches in the plastic cartridge, and there is no winding back at the end of the film.

Viewfinder information

As the camera is fully automatic there is no need for detailed exposure information. There are therefore only two LEDs—a green one which indicates that there is enough light for hand-held photography, and a yellow one warning that there is not. Exposure is still calculated automatically when the yellow LED is lit, but the camera must be mounted on a tripod; alternatively one of the dedicated flash units may be fitted.

The focusing screen is similar to the standard 35mm SLR type: there is a central split-image spot surrounded by an overall matt field.

Pentax 6 × 7 system

Rollfilm SLR with optional TTL zero-method open-aperture exposure metering. The Pentax 6 × 7 is a comprehensive professional system which combines 35mm convenience with rollfilm quality—image area is 55 × 70mm, which, being rectangular, makes better use of the emulsion area than the 6cm (2¼in) square format, as this almost invariably has to be cropped. Based on the standard 35mm SLR design, the 6 × 7 system features eye-level pentaprism viewing and a complete system of interchangeable lenses; it achieves maximum portability for the format.

The system consists of the following.

Pentax 6 × 7 body

Interchangeable viewfinders

Five interchangeable focusing screens

Seventeen interchangeable lenses as follows:

Fish-eye: 35mm f/4.5

Wide-angle: 45mm f/4, 55mm f/4, 75mm f/4.5, 75mm f/4.5 Shift

Standard: 90mm f/2.8, 90mm f/2.8 Leaf Shutter Lens; 105mm f/2.4

Telephoto: 150mm f/2.8, 200mm f/4, 300mm f/4, 400mm, 500mm, 600mm, 800mm, 1000mm

Macro: 135mm f/4

Further accessories (for descriptions refer to the equivalent 35mm accessories listed on page 141-144): Auto Extension Set (3-piece); Extension Tube Set (2-piece); Auto Bellows; Helicoid Extension Tube; Slide copier; 49mm and 67mm Reverse Adaptors; Slide Holder K; Rear Converter T6-2X; Copy Stand; Right-angle Finder; Correction Lenses; Magnifier (for critical focusing); Eyecup; Close-up Lenses; Grip; various lens hoods, filters, mount adaptors and cases.

Summary of Pentax camera features

▒ shaded areas show features present.

	LX	ME SUPER	ME-F	MG	K1000	MX
Automatic exposure features						
Automatic exposure	■	■	■	■		
Exposure compensation facility	■	■	■	■		
Manual override	■	■	■			
Stepless electronic shutter control	■	■	■	■		
Camera facilities						
'B' setting	■	■	■		■	■
Shutter cocked indicator	■	■	■	■		■
Exposure lock	■	■	■			
Self-timer	■	■	■	■		■
Multiple exposure facility	■					■
Exposure counter	■	■	■	■	■	■
Depth of field preview	■					■
Mirror lock	■					
Magic needle loading	■	■	■	■		
Memo holder	■	■	■	■		
Film transport indicator	■	■	■	■		
Batteryless operation	■				■	■
Interchangeable parts						
Interchangeable lenses	■	■	■	■	■	■
Interchangeable viewfinders	■					
Interchangeable focusing screens	■					■
Interchangeable data back	■	■				
Exposure metering functions						
TTL exposure metering	■	■	■	■	■	■
Centre-weighted metering	■	■	■	■	■	■
Automatic meter shut-off	■	■	■	■		
IDM metering	■					
Flash						
Hot shoe	■	■	■	■	■	■
X-synch socket	■	■	■			■
TTL flash metering	■					
Dedicated flash facility	■	■	■	■		
Motorized functions						
Motor winder	■	■	■	■		■
Motor drive	■					■

48

6 The Pentax ME Super

An aperture-priority automatic 35mm SLR with full manual override. It offers both innovations and improvements in specifications over previous Pentax models and over current models from other manufacturers in the same price band.

The innovations

The revolutionary features which set the ME Super apart from all other cameras with the solitary exception of its legendary predecessor the ME, lie in the dual 'shutter-dial-less' exposure systems with electropulse manual speed selection. The 3-colour LED display in the viewfinder is also innovative, containing no less than 18 LEDs supplying a constant stream of essential information (but tucked over to one side so as not to hamper picture composition).

The improvements

While this camera continues the tradition established in previous Pentax cameras of combining advanced performance with light weight and small size, the miniaturization of its electronics has made space available for the development of other benefits.

For example, electronic shutter speed control runs over the entire range from 4 sec to 1/2000 sec, on manual as well as automatic; this top speed is unprecedented in so small a camera.

The mirror is equipped with a new specially cushioned return action for exceptional quietness and freedom from vibration.

The body has been redesigned to sit even more comfortably in the hands, while the controls, though highly responsive, are easily operated even by people with large fingers.

The 3-way focusing screen has a new coating to improve light transmission; focusing and composing the picture are even easier than before.

There are other improvements, not all of which can be seen by the user. As science makes new, more durable materials available to industry these are investigated by the Asahi Optical Company and adopted where they offer increased strength or reliability. Other improvements such as the enlarged air damper are concealed by the construction of the camera, but are there nevertheless.

Preparing the ME Super for use

The new ME Super camera body and the lens of your choice are packaged separately. The box containing the body also contains:

Body cap (fitted)   Tripod spacer
Finder cap (fitted)   Instruction manual
2 alkaline batteries

All new Pentax lenses are supplied with a protective cap at each end.

The following steps simply prepare the new ME Super for snapshooting and in no way reveal the full potential of this versatile camera.

Mounting the lens

Unwrap the ME Super body and the lens, and remove the caps from the body and the back of the lens. Keep these caps in a safe place.

Align the red spot just inside the flange on the bayonet mounting of the lens with the identical red spot on the receiving plate of the camera body. Insert the lens into the body and turn it clockwise until it locks—this takes less than one-quarter turn. The whole operation is remarkably simple.

Inserting the batteries

Two alkaline batteries are supplied with the camera. When unpacking, take care to handle them only by the edges, as fingerprinting can cause poor contact. Wipe them with a dry cloth such as a clean handkerchief or tissue before insertion.

The battery chamber is located next to the tripod socket in the base of the camera body, and the cover can be unscrewed with a coin. Put the batteries into the chamber one on top of the other with the + mark on the flat side facing down. Replace the cover and screw tight.

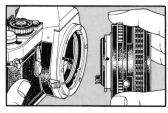

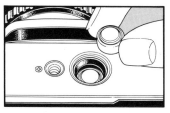

The first steps in preparing a new ME Super for use — (above) inserting the batteries; (above left) mounting the lens. To remove the lens, reverse the procedure, pressing the lens release button with the thumb.

To check that batteries are correctly inserted and active, set the exposure mode dial to AUTO or M, and press lightly on the shutter button while looking through the viewfinder. At least one of the LEDs should light up and glow continuously for about 30 seconds. If the 2000 and 4S LEDs flash on and off battery power is low and both batteries will soon need to be replaced. Any other LEDs that flicker can be ignored at this stage as they are designed to do so in certain circumstances. If no LED lights at all this indicates that batteries are either dead or not correctly inserted.

Setting the exposure mode dial
Depress the white index button on the rim of the dial and turn until the indicator stands at 125×. (This is simply because if the camera is on AUTO and the lens cap is on or the light is poor, the 3-4 'dummy' exposures required to bring the first frame to the film gate will be unnecessarily long in duration.)

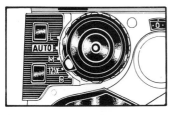

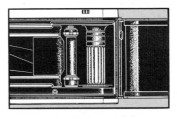

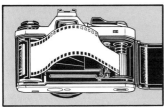

Film loading (left) is very easy due to the simplicity of the Pentax 'magic needle' loading system (above): just insert the leader between any two of the white rods. Do this with the exposure mode dial at 125× (above left).

Loading the film
This should be carried out in subdued light. Use the shade of your own body if film has to be loaded outdoors in direct sun.

To open the camera, pull up on the rewind knob until the back springs loose. If the camera is new remove the protective plastic cover from the pressure plate. Place the cassette in the film chamber on the left, with the trimmed leader extending over the lower guide rail, then push the rewind knob down, rotating it *slightly* if necessary to get the shaft to engage in the film spool.

Insert the tip of the film leader between any two of the white rods (the 'magic needles') on the take-up spool. Pull enough film out of the cassette to be able to do this comfortably; film manufacturers make a generous allowance for this procedure and it will not result in wasted frames. Wind the film on with the film advance lever, releasing the shutter as necessary, until the film perforations are engaged top and bottom by the sprocket wheel. Close the camera back and press it firmly to lock. Continue to advance the film and release the shutter alternately until frame no. 1 is indicated in the exposure counter window. To check that film is correctly loaded, watch the transport indicator: this should oscillate in the window as film is advanced. The rewind knob should also turn anticlockwise, but this movement is often irregular because of slack in the cassette.

Setting the film speed and exposure compensation dials

The ASA scale only is used on the ME Super. To set the film speed raise the collar around the dial and turn until the required ASA number appears in the window opposite the orange index mark.

Let the collar fall back into position and turn the entire dial assembly until the 1× on the exposure compensation dial is aligned with the orange index pointer next to the pentaprism housing.

When you first start to use the ME Super, choose an aperture according to the table: for this situation probably f/11 or f/22.

	Film speed (ASA)		
	25-100	100-200	200-400
Sun	f/11	f/16	f/22
Light cloud	f/8	f/11	f/16
Heavy cloud	f/4-5.6	f/5.6-8	f/8-11
Indoors	f/1.4-2	f/2-2.8	f/2.8-4

Setting the AUTO exposure mode

Turn the dial until the indicator is at AUTO, in which position it will be locked until the white index button is depressed. The ME Super is now ready for action.

Setting the lens aperture

Aperture is adjusted by means of the inner ring on the lens. Turn the ring until the required f/number is aligned with the diamond index mark in front of it, on the fixed part of the lens barrel.

It will simplify handling in the early stages, while you are still getting accustomed to the feel of the camera, if you preselect an aperture according to the table above.

Framing and focusing

Select a subject and focus the lens by rotating the ring at the front. The ME Super is equipped with a 3-way focusing screen (as described on page 32) and focusing is a very simple matter. Look in the viewfinder and check *either* that any line on the subject passing through the central circle is unbroken, *or* that there is no flickering in parts of the subject lying within the surrounding microprism collar, *or* that the image is sharp and clear in the overall viewfinder field.

Exposure check

Lightly pressing the shutter release button activates the LED display in the viewfinder, and this remains illuminated for about 30 seconds, regardless of whether finger pressure is maintained or an exposure made.

If the preparations detailed previously have been thoroughly carried out, one of the green LEDs should glow. This indicates that shutter speed will be between 1/60 and 1/2000 sec, and that it is safe to go ahead and shoot.

A full description of the viewfinder LED display is given on page 54. The following notes are for *quick reference only*, in case a green LED does not show in the viewfinder at the first attempt.

IF a yellow LED shows in the viewfinder, indicating that shutter speed will be between 4 secs and 1/30 sec. . .

·THEN keeping your eye to the viewfinder, rotate the aperture setting ring anticlockwise (to a lower f/number) until a green LED shows, then shoot.

| EF |
| M |
| OVER |
| 2000 |
| 1000 |
| 500 |
| 250 |
| 125X |
| 60 |
| 30 |
| 15 |
| 8 |
| 4 |
| 2 |
| 1 |
| 2s |
| 4s |
| UNDER |

IF the red 'OVER' LED glows. . .

THEN turn the aperture setting ring clockwise (to a higher f/number) until a green LED begins to show, then shoot.

IF the red 'UNDER' LED glows. . .

THEN turn the aperture setting ring anticlockwise (to a lower f/number) until a green LED begins to show; if maximum aperture is reached before this happens there is not enough light for hand-held photography. The solution is to use a faster film, support the camera on a tripod and shoot when a yellow LED shows, or use flash.

To make the exposure

Press the shutter button all the way down. The image in the viewfinder will black out momentarily and there will be an audible click. Advance the film in readiness for the next shot.

Interpretation of LEDs

Where relevant, remedial action is printed in *italic script*.

Colour	Label	LED glows continuously	LED flashes on and off
Red	EF		Exposure factor is in use: *if not required set dial to 1 ×*
Green	M	Camera is in manual mode	Dedicated flash unit is charged and ready to fire
Red	OVER	Camera is on AUTO and aperture is too wide: *stop down until LED goes out*	Camera is on Manual and picture will be overexposed: *stop down* or *increase shutter speed until LED goes out*
Green	2000	1/2000 sec ⎫	Batteries weak: *replace both*
Green	1000	1/1000 sec ⎪	
Green	500	1/500 sec ⎪	
Green	250	1/250 sec ⎬ Shoot	
Green	125×	1/125 sec Also indicates shutter is synchronized with dedicated flash unit ⎪	
Green	60	1/60 sec ⎭	
Yellow	30	1/30 sec ⎫ Shutter	
Yellow	15	1/15 sec ⎪ speed too	
Yellow	8	1/8 sec ⎪ slow for hand-held shooting:	
Yellow	4	1/4 sec ⎪	
Yellow	2	1/2 sec ⎬ *open up aperture* or	
Yellow	1	1 sec ⎪ *use a tripod*	
Yellow	2S	2 secs ⎪ or *use flash*	
Yellow	4S	4 secs ⎭ or *use faster film*	Batteries weak: *replace both*
Red	UNDER	Camera is on AUTO and aperture is too small: *open up until LED goes out, then proceed as indicated for yellow LEDs*	Camera is on Manual and pictures will be underexposed: *open up aperture* or *decrease shutter speed until LED goes out*

N.B. If no LED shows when shutter button is pressed it is due to one of the following:
Exposure mode dial is set to 125×, B or L
Batteries are dead, missing or wrongly inserted

Holding the camera

In hand-held photography it is vital to achieve maximum stability; and this applies to the whole body, not just to the hands. Any movement of the camera during exposure will cause loss of picture sharpness. This is an aspect of photography that can easily become neglected, so it pays to develop good habits early on.

Stand comfortably with the feet not too far apart, elbows not sticking out and body *definitely not* leaning back (if you find you are too close to a subject move your feet away from it, not just your body from the waist up). Sometimes it is necessary to kneel or lie down, stand precariously on various objects to gain extra height, and so on. In awkward situations a fast shutter speed should be used.

For static subjects the camera may be held with the hands gripping the sides symmetrically except for the forefinger on the shutter button, focus and aperture having been adjusted previously. But when working at speed or with long lenses the left hand should support the camera body, with the thumb and forefinger on the lens poised to adjust the focusing and aperture rings at a moment's notice.

For vertical framing the camera can be turned on either side according to personal preference, but the left hand should still provide as much support as possible to the lens. Keep the elbows well in, particularly among crowds.

Tripods and many other types of support are widely available and should always be used for slow shutter speeds. At intermediate speeds —around 1/15 sec—the extra stability that can be gained by leaning against a vertical object such as a lamp post or tree, or resting the elbows on a solid surface such as a wall or table, *may* be enough to prevent camera shake spoiling the picture. Every individual has to work out his own capabilities.

Changing lenses

The Pentax K bayonet mounting system was originally designed to facilitate the process of changing lenses for photographers working in the field; it is completed very quickly, even in total darkness or with the camera in a bag.

To remove the fitted lens, hold the camera in the left hand and depress the lens release lever with the thumb. With the right hand turn the lens anticlockwise until it is released (less than one-quarter turn). Cover the rear element with a protective cap as soon as possible: use the one from the lens you are fitting to the camera.

The normal lens mounting procedure is described on page 50. To mount a lens with the camera in a bag, or when the light is too low for the red spots to be seen, locate the raised white node on the lens barrel with the thumb of the right hand and align it with the lens release lever on the camera body. Insert the lens and turn clockwise to lock as normal. If you expect to have to do this, practice a few times with your eyes closed.

Rewinding and unloading the film

When the last frame on a roll of film has been exposed the film cannot be advanced any further. Do not exert undue force on the film advance lever.

The film must be rewound into its cassette before being unloaded. Depress the film rewind button in the base plate of the camera, lift out the rewind crank and turn clockwise until the film disengages from the

Holding the camera. Top left – the standard method for most shots, with the left hand ready to adjust focusing and aperture rings. Top right and centre left – vertical shots can be framed with the camera turned on either side, whichever you find more comfortable. Left – supporting a longer lens, in this case a one-touch zoom. Above – lean against a solid surface such as a wall or tree trunk for extra stability.

sprockets and take-up spool: there will be a definite slackening of resistance on the crank when this happens. Give a few more turns to wind the leader back into the cassette: if you do this there is no danger of mistaking an exposed film for an unexposed one. Pull upwards on the rewind knob to open the camera back, lift out the cassette, and have it processed as soon as possible; until then it should be stored in a cool dark place.

The ME Super: other facilities and their use

Memo holder

Each time a new film is loaded, unless it is identical to the previous one, the top can be torn off the box and inserted into the memo holder on the camera back. This serves as a reminder of film type and is particularly useful for people who often change from one type of film to another, and for people who tend to put the camera away loaded for long periods of time (which is not recommended as film should be processed as soon as possible after exposure). It is sometimes useful to add other information such as date and/or location of loading; and certainly make a note of it if the film is being underexposed with a view to push processing.

The self-timer

To operate the self-timer push the lever down, away from the lens, until it stops, which is at an angle of just over 90° from the vertical. Slight upward pressure on the lever will start the cycle. This lasts about 10 seconds and is accompanied by a whirring noise which continues for a few more seconds after exposure.

This delay enables the photographer to get himself into the picture. Obviously the camera must be on a tripod or similar support, and the shutter must be cocked.

The self-timer can be used with the camera in either the automatic or the manual mode, or on 125×. If used on automatic, the viewfinder cap should be fitted in order to prevent light entering the camera from the back and influencing the meter to underexpose.

In certain circumstances where hand-held shooting with slow shutter speeds is unavoidable, releasing the shutter by means of the self-timer can help to reduce camera shake: the photographer does not need to exert downward pressure on the shutter button at the moment of exposure and can concentrate on holding the camera steady with both hands.

Double or multiple exposures

Deliberate double or multiple exposure can lead to some interesting effects. The first exposure should be made normally. To cock the shutter for a second or subsequent exposure on to the same frame, tighten the film by turning the rewind crank clockwise and holding it in position to prevent the film from advancing; then depress the film rewind button underneath the camera as you cock the shutter with the film advance lever. The camera is now ready for the second exposure.

The exposures may not be exactly superimposed by this method, so leave one frame blank before resuming normal photography; note also that the exposure counter will be out of step by as many additional exposures as you make.

The more times any single frame is exposed the more the total light value accumulates on it. A degree of underexposure may therefore improve the final picture, depending on subject illumination.

Operation without batteries

The ME Super can be used without batteries if the exposure mode dial is set to AUTO, 125× or B. (1/125 is a good average working speed for most purposes; on AUTO the shutter speed is about 1/1000 sec.) As the exposure meter will not be working the tables given in film manufacturers' leaflets should be consulted, applying the reciprocity law if speeds other than 1/125 sec are quoted. The following is a guide which can be used if no leaflets are to hand.

Use of the camera on the B setting is the same with or without batteries: see page 76. (You would need a hand-held meter.)

Set camera to 125×	Film speed (ASA)			
	25-50	50-100	100-200	200-400
Bright sun; snow or sand	f/11	f/16	f/22	f/11 on AUTO
Bright sun elsewhere	f/8	f/11	f/16	f/22
Hazy sun	f/5.6	f/8	f/11	f/16
Heavy cloud	f/2.8	f/4	f/5.6	f/8
Indoors	—	Max.	f/2	f/2.8

Note that indoor lighting varies so much in intensity that it is impossible to guarantee correct exposure by means of a chart. The results obtained may be acceptable if it is very important to record the occasion.

Stop-down metering

The great majority of Pentax SMC lenses have a diaphragm coupling lever which provides a direct link between the aperture setting ring and the light meter/shutter control circuitry. It is this link that makes open-aperture metering possible.

In some ultra-telephoto lenses and certain other accessories fitted between lens and camera body, because of design limitations imposed by their physical complexity, it is not practical to incorporate a diaphragm coupler. In these cases the iris diaphragm is activated manually by rotation of the aperture setting ring, and the meter controls the LED display and shutter speed without further modification.

The procedure for taking pictures is exactly the same as for open-aperture metering; however, as the lens is stopped down the image in the viewfinder becomes progressively darker. With small apertures, therefore, it may be necessary to frame the shot before stopping down.

The lenses and accessories with which it is necessary to use the stop-down metering system are as follows. SMC Pentax lenses: 500mm f/4.5; 1000mm f/8; Reflex 1000mm f/11; Reflex 2000m f/13.5; Zoom 135-600mm f/6.7; Shift 28mm f/3.5, and Bellows 100mm f/4 when used with Bellows Unit M. Accessories: Extension Tube Set K; Helicoid Extension Tube K; Reverse Adaptor K and Bellows Unit K.

Care and maintenance

The Pentax ME Super is designed as a working photographer's camera and as such it does not need to be handled like a piece of eggshell china. But like any other instrument containing precision-engineered mechanisms it is more likely to sustain damage if dropped, knocked against hard surfaces or otherwise treated to excessive violence. It should always be handled in accordance with the dictates of common sense, and preferably kept in a Pentax case or bag.

Dirt or smudges on the optics will cause loss of image quality. Use a protective lens cap when the camera is not in use, and preferably keep an ultraviolet filter permanently in place on the lens—this will have no adverse effect on any of your photographs, and in the event of impact with a hard or sharp object it is cheaper to replace a filter than the lens. Lenses not in use should be protected with caps front and rear, and preferably kept in individual cases.

Dust the outer surfaces of lenses and filters from time to time, using a blower brush to blow off loose matter before brushing. Hold the part being cleaned upside down so that particles of dust and grit fall away from, rather than into, the mechanisms. If such particles are wiped around the lens elements with a cloth they can scratch the surfaces, so dust thoroughly *before* wiping off smudges, fingerprints etc. Use a clean cloth such as a lens tissue or a cotton handkerchief (clean but not new). Commercial lens cleaning fluids can be used.

Occasional blower-brushing inside the camera body between films will help to preserve the mechanisms against the attacks of dust. Be very careful not to touch the mirror, focusing screen, shutter blinds (from either side) or the pressure plate with your fingers. Dust and marks on the mirror and focusing screen will not affect your photographs no matter how disfiguring they look in the viewfinder.

Water, and particularly salt water and spray, can cause serious damage to optics and corrosion in camera mechanisms. Surface splashes should be mopped off without delay, and if the camera becomes completely immersed in water it should be taken immediately to the nearest authorized Pentax service centre.

A camera left lying in direct sun will become very hot and the electronics may be permanently damaged. Sand and probing little fingers can be equally destructive in their own way.

If a camera has to be stored for any length of time remove lens and batteries and cover openings with protective caps. Store away from places where temperature and humidity may fluctuate more than a little; cool, dry, dust-free but well ventilated place is best. Pack a bag of silica gel with the body and one in each lens case—these will absorb moisture from the air and help to protect equipment from damp. Finish any film that is in the camera: the emulsion deteriorates more quickly after exposure than before.

For shorter term storage keep the camera in its case or bag, but still away from extremes of temperature or humidity.

Working temperatures

The ME Super and other cameras in the Pentax range are capable of functioning normally at any temperature between −20°C (−4°F) and

50°C (122°F), and not one in a hundred users will find this range too narrow. However, the following precautions should be observed.

If the camera is to be used in very cold conditions it should be overhauled and the oil replaced by an authorized Pentax agent.

Sudden changes of temperature may cause condensation to form in the camera. If the moisture subsequently freezes the droplets expand and can cause damage to the intricate internal mechanisms; if it does not freeze it can cause rust instead, which may be just as harmful in the long run. Therefore gradual acclimatization is necessary: break the temperature change up into stages of about 10°C (20°F) or so, allowing about 30 minutes for each stage.

Battery performance is impaired by extreme cold. Keep the batteries out of the camera until you are ready to shoot, and keep at least one spare pair of batteries ready in your kit.

7 Using the ME Super on AUTO

'Two cameras in one. So easy . . . but so professional' is how the ME Super has been described in a glossy publicity brochure issued by the Asahi Optical Company. This statement in fact undersells the product and in so doing propagates a myth about automatic exposure control which should, by now, have been universally discredited. The ME Super, set in its aperture-priority automatic mode, can, it is true, be used as a snapshooting camera by people who lack either the time or the inclination to learn more about photography. This is the 'so easy' camera of the slogan; the photographs it delivers will be beautifully exposed, with a razor-edged bite to the focus, full and saturated colour, and will be a credit to the camera.

The problem is that this side of automatic exposure is often given the hard sell at the expense of the more serious side. The fact is, when a photographer has learned to make full use of the automatic exposure function, it can enable him to bring in images which would otherwise have got away. And is this not the real reason for investing in a sophisticated camera and not just a good lens?

The principal benefit of automatic exposure control is speed. Many images, especially those with people in them, are only fleetingly available before the composition breaks up or the subjects notice the camera and alter their behaviour or become self-conscious. In these situations the time it takes to adjust the controls may make the difference between capturing the image or missing it for good. There is much more to it than this, though, as will become clear in due course.

Setting the camera

For automatic exposure control the exposure mode dial must be set to AUTO, the film speed must be correctly set, with the exposure compensation dial at 1×.

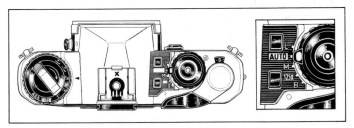

Total control with the aperture ring

Ambient light levels are not the only consideration affecting the choice of aperture for automatic exposure: the table given on page 52 is only a beginning. The next step is to decide what kind of image you are planning or what type of photography you are about to embark on. (Although presented here as a sequence of steps, the whole decision-making process does become more of an instinctive reaction than a conscious one.)

Broadly speaking, there are three alternatives:

(i) Rapid-reaction situations, i.e. where images may present themselves without any warning, then vanish with equal suddeness. This is the subject matter of much photojournalism, but moments of humour in family life, or holiday scenes, especially where children are involved, can call for the same speed of response and require the same range of camera skills.

(ii) Subjects which are static but which either extend over a considerable depth (and therefore necessitate the use of relatively small apertures to ensure adequate depth of field) or which you wish to isolate from their background by means of differential focusing (and therefore necessitate the use of wide apertures).

(iii) Moving subjects, the final appearance of which will be governed more by shutter speed than by lens aperture.

Rapid-reaction situations

There is a surprising amount that can be done to a camera in advance of going out on location, reducing the actual shooting procedure to a bare minimum. In fact, if the camera is to be used in reasonably good daylight the whole picture-taking process can be turned into a compose-and-shoot operation, so that virtually the only variables determining whether the picture will be good are the photographer's eye and his timing.

First, choose a fast film—400 ASA, not less. This makes it possible to use smaller apertures, and hence increases depth of field; this in turn makes fine focusing less critical.

Take a number of exposure readings and work out from them an average aperture that will keep the shutter speed in the 1/60-1/125 sec range—i.e. as slow as is safe in hand-held photography, with a small safety margin. On a fine day the aperture should be around f/16.

Work out the *hyperfocal distance* (see below) and set the focusing ring to this distance; use the scale engraved on the lens, ignoring the focusing aids in the viewfinder. At f/16 with a standard 50mm lens the hyperfocal distance is 5.2m (16ft), and when the lens is focused on this distance everything will be in focus from 2.6m (8ft)—or half the hyperfocal distance—to infinity. As long as there is no important subject matter closer than 2.6m you can shoot without a second thought whenever you have an interesting subject in the viewfinder. There is no need to waste time adjusting anything on the camera.

Each time an exposure is made the shutter speed will be displayed in the viewfinder. If this begins to fall into the yellow LED range on account of failing light, open up a stop and work out the new hyperfocal distance.

Auto exposure and depth of field

As far as regulating depth of field is concerned, with automatic exposure it is possible to achieve the same results as with manual exposure—no more and no less—but in considerably less time. Focusing distance remains an important factor, as does the focal length of the lens in use.

To maximize depth of field, simply activate the exposure meter and turn the aperture ring until the green LED marked 60 lights up, indicating that shutter speed will be around the 1/60 second mark. The aperture will then be as small as is compatible with hand-held photography. By all means go down to 1/30 sec if you have a very steady hand, but remember that under electronic control the speeds are stepless and can be half a stop or so

In situations like this you do not have time to ponder: work out the hyperfocal distance beforehand and shoot on AUTO.

slower than indicated by the LEDs. If the only way to obtain adequate depth of field is to use a shutter speed in the yellow LED range, then the camera will need to be mounted on a tripod or equally firm support.

The reverse procedure will naturally minimize depth of field, so if differential focusing is required in order to make a subject stand out from a distracting background, rotate the aperture ring anticlockwise until either the maximum aperture of the lens is reached or a shutter speed of 1/2000 sec is indicated.

At any aperture, depth of field extends a certain distance behind the exact point focused on and a certain distance in front of it. If the lens is focused on infinity (∞) this capacity for sharp focus beyond the exact focusing distance is not being used.

The distance at which the lens should be focused in order to obtain maximum depth of field is known as the *hyperfocal distance*. When a lens is focused at this distance, the far limit of sharp focus is infinity and the near limit is half the hyperfocal distance.

To work out the hyperfocal distance is not complicated: it is the near limit of sharpness with the lens focused on infinity. For any given aperture, the near limit of depth of field can be read from a table or from the depth of field scale on the lens barrel. Focus the lens on this distance, and that is all there is to it. You will observe that the infinity symbol is aligned with the relevant f/number on the depth of field scale to the left of the index mark; the distance aligned with the same f/number on the right of the index mark indicates the near limit of depth of field. Therefore, focusing the lens by aligning the ∞ symbol against the f/number in use is another way of achieving the same result.

Focusing on the hyperfocal distance is an extremely useful technique to employ in situations where the rapid reactions necessary to grab the best shots leave little time for camera adjustments. However, its usefulness diminishes sharply at lower f/numbers and with longer lenses. The following table, giving hyperfocal distances for 50mm and 35mm lenses at various apertures, may be helpful.

50mm lens			35mm lens		
	Hyperfocal	*Near limit*		*Hyperfocal*	*Near limit*
f/no.	*distance*	*of focus*	*f/no.*	*distance*	*of focus*
22	3.8m (12½ft)	1.9m (6ft)	22	1.8m (6ft)	0.9m (3ft)
16	5.2m (17ft)	2.6m (8½ft)	16	2.6m (8½ft)	1.3m (4ft)
11	7.5m (25ft)	3.8m (12½ft)	11	3.7m (12ft)	1.8m (6ft)
8	10.4m (34ft)	5.2m (17ft)	8	5.1m (17ft)	2.6m (8½ft)
5.6	14.9m (49ft)	7.4m (25ft)	5.6	7.3m (24ft)	3.6m (12ft)
4	21.0m (69ft)	10.0m (33ft)	4	10.2m (35ft)	5.1m (17ft)
			2.8	16.6m (50ft)	7.3m (25ft)

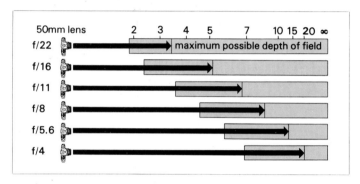

Auto exposure and subject movement

The photographer has always had the option of 'freezing' motion or deliberately letting it (or the background) become blurred. This option is retained even with aperture-priority automatic exposure, as long as shutter speed is indicated in the viewfinder—as it is in the ME Super. The technique may appear illogical at first, but it is perfectly straightforward: treat the aperture ring as a shutter speed control; forget about f/numbers and observe only the shutter speeds indicated by the LEDs.

The only way in which this differs from manual shutter speed selection is that the actual exposure time may vary from the indicated time, either because of the stepless nature of the electronic control system, or because of a sudden change in lighting conditions. In the first case, any departure from the indicated speed will almost certainly not make any discernible difference to the photograph—the normal scale of speeds is after all a quite arbitary if logical progression: fixed steps of 1/30 or 1/60 sec have no arcane importance of their own. In the second case, a sudden change in lighting conditions which causes an automated change of shutter speed would, in manual systems, lead instead to a wrong exposure; the slight uncertainty about actual shutter speed is surely a small sacrifice to make for *guaranteed* correct exposure.

Using a fast film on a reasonably bright day you can freeze
subject movement by choosing a wide aperture.

Long exposures on AUTO

Automatic shutter speed control goes down to and beyond the lower
limit of manual speeds (4 secs). If the LED read-out in the viewfinder
flickers between 4S and UNDER, or if you find that introducing a brighter
object (such as your hand) temporarily into the image area alters the read-
out from UNDER to 4S, indicating that shutter speed is nearly but not
quite within the marked range, it is safe to shoot on automatic.

There are three points to remember when making long exposures on
AUTO, the first of which is obvious: for exposures of this duration a tripod
must be used and the shutter released by cable or by the use of the selftimer.

The second is less obvious: light entering the camera body through the
viewfinder eyepiece will affect the exposure meter, and hence shutter
speed, unless blocked at the moment the shutter is released. The photographer's head blocks the viewfinder in normal hand-held photography, but
when using a tripod and cable release he will probably be standing back.
It is specifically for use in this situation that a viewfinder cap is supplied
with every new body. (N.B. there is no danger of light that enters the
camera through the viewfinder actually reaching the film.)

The third point relates to the breakdown of the reciprocity law (see page
23) at exposures of longer than 1 second or so. With colour reversal
emulsions designed for short exposures of 1/2 sec or less, the effect of
prolonged exposure times is unpredictable. However, it is known that
their ASA rating is reduced, and that an additional increase in exposure is
necessary to overcome this. Preferably open up the aperture to effect an
increase of $\frac{1}{2}$ stop for exposures up to about 3 secs, and 1 stop for exposures
up to 10 secs.

Colour	Label	If CORRECT EXPOSURE alone, or SPEED OF SHOOTING is the overriding factor, and for simple snapshots
Red	EF	
Green	M	
Red	OVER	Stop down until LED goes out and is replaced by a green one
Green	2000	Shoot
Green	1000	Shoot
Green	500	Shoot
Green	250	Shoot
Green	125×	Shoot
Green	60	Shoot
Yellow	30	Open up aperture until a green LED lights, or shoot on yellow taking precautions against camera shake; with suitable subjects use flash
Yellow	15	
Yellow	8	
Yellow	4	
Yellow	2	
Yellow	1	
Yellow	2S	
Yellow	4S	
Red	UNDER	Open up aperture until LED goes out and is replaced by a yellow one, then follow procedure for yellow LEDs

If you stop to worry about camera controls the canoeist will be gone: shoot if a green LED is showing.

If MAXIMUM DEPTH OF FIELD is required together with variable focusing, or if a SLOW SHUTTER SPEED is required	If DIFFERENTIAL FOCUSING is required (conditions permitting) or a FAST SHUTTER SPEED is wanted in order to freeze motion
Stop down as far as possible without going into the yellow LED range	Stop down only as far as necessary to illuminate a green LED
	Shoot
Stop down as far as possible without illuminating a yellow LED	Open up to maximum aperture or as far as possible without causing red OVER LED to light
Shoot	
Open up aperture only as far as necessary to illuminate a green LED; if light is too poor to take LEDs into green range at maximum aperture, take precautions against camera shake. For static subjects shoot on yellow but using a tripod.	Open up to maximum aperture or as far as possible without causing red OVER LED to light. If light is too poor to take LEDs into green range at maximum aperture, take precautions against camera shake
Open up aperture until LED goes out and is replaced by a yellow one, then follow procedure for yellow LEDS	Open up aperture as far as possible. If light is too poor to take LEDs into the green range at maximum aperture, take precautions against camera shake

Open up the aperture as far as you can, stopping before the red 'OVER' LED begins to glow, for an out-of-focus background.

Exposure compensation

One of the open secrets of success in automatic photography is to learn to recognize lighting conditions in which the objective analysis provided by the built-in light meter can be 'improved' by human intervention. These conditions fall into three broad categories. The first consists of subjects in which the contrast is too great for photographic emulsions to handle. The second consists of subjects in which there is a preponderance of very light or very dark tones. The third category consists of subjects which, in the photographer's opinion, would benefit from being manipulated rather than recorded straight, so as to be made to appear lighter or darker in the photograph than they actually were in reality.

High-contrast subjects

If the image area contains both very bright and densely shaded areas there is bound to be a loss of detail in one or the other. The film emulsion itself lacks the means to record detail in both, so no meter can provide a universal solution. The situation is made particularly insidious by the fact that the human eye is sensitive to a broader bandwidth of luminosity than film, and often does not perceive the signals warning that there are, photographically speaking, special forces at work. Since they do not impinge upon our consciousness, we must be ready to turn the stones over looking for them.

Typically, the situation arises when an object or person is photographed against a highly luminous background such as a window or the sky, or in a snowbound landscape, or against a sunlit backdrop such as a beach in the summer. These can be brighter than they look to human eyes, and their

This scene contains both interior and exterior subject matter; the photographer chose to expose for the shaded area: notice how the highlights have burnt out.

brightness tends to 'pull' the meter in such a way that it will underexpose the real subject.

The reverse situation occurs when the background is very dark: if the meter reads this it will tend to overexpose the relatively bright parts of the subject. Spotlit faces on a dark stage, telephoto shots of the moon, stained glass windows in a dark building and city lights at night are all examples of this kind of subject.

The rule is: if the background is very bright, then keep it bright—*over*expose by turning the dial to 2× or 4×. If the background is very dark, then keep it dark—*under*expose by turning the dial to $\frac{1}{2}$× or $\frac{1}{4}$×.

To work out whether the exposure factor should be one stop or two, choose a part of the subject which represents approximately average illumination and go in close enough to fill the viewfinder with this detail. It does not matter about focusing, so go in as close as you need to without casting a shadow on to the area being metered. Compare the reading taken at this distance with the one taken from the shooting position, and compensate by the difference; e.g if the whole subject illuminates the green 1000 LED and a detail reading illuminates the 250 LED, you need to overexpose by 2 stops, hence 4×. Not all subjects can be selectively metered in this way—a close-up reading of the moon might involve an effort that even the most dedicated photographer would consider disproportionate—so until you are experienced enough to be able to estimate the compensation factor, either play safe by bracketing exposure (see below) or use a hand-held spot meter (page 144). On occasion, 2 stops may be inadequate to compensate for the extreme conditions, in which case the exposure has to be made manually.

Atypical subjects

All TTL meters measure reflected light. Black surfaces reflect little or none of the light that falls on them. White surfaces reflect nearly all of it, but there may not be much to reflect. From this it follows that a TTL meter is absolutely oblivious to the differences between a black surface in bright light, a grey or medium-coloured surface in low light and a white surface that is not lit at all: from all three it receives the same message and converts it to the same exposure value. If the f/stops and shutter speeds derived from this are used, images in which light and dark areas are more or less evenly balanced—the great majority of all photographs—will be correctly exposed, as will average subjects under soft, even illumination. But images in which black or dark-coloured areas occupy most of the area will be misread as average subjects that are poorly lit, and they will be made to come out grey. Images in which white or pale-coloured areas predominate will be misread as average subjects that are brilliantly illuminated—and will also be made to come out grey.

In these cases the photographer must restore the imbalance of nature, *under*exposing dark or black subjects ($\frac{1}{2}$× or $\frac{1}{4}$× on the dial) and *over*exposing white or pale subjects (2× or 4×). Working out how many stops to compensate by is, again, a matter of experience. However, taking a light measurement from a piece of grey card and setting an exposure factor equivalent to the difference between this and a measurement from the subject will usually give very accurate results (but make sure the grey card is lit from the same source as the subject).

Interpreted images

Sometimes a photographer may wish to alter theoretically correct exposure for creative reasons. Overexposure, which normally results in thin images and washed out colours, can be used deliberately to create a delicate, ethereal impression or a bright and airy 'high key' effect. Underexposure can lead to strong colour saturation; otherwise 'low key' effects may be sombre or serious or may invoke an atmosphere of Stygian gloom.

Bracketing exposures

The term bracketing refers to the practice of making a number of exposures of a given subject instead of a single one, each at a slightly different setting. This is very sound practice if there is any doubt about the exact nature of the lighting, or if the subject is of particular importance (a wedding group, for example). Many photographers bracket all their static shots as a matter of course, and sometimes, quite unexpectedly, find that an under or overexposed one depicts the subject with more 'insight' than the shot they had planned.

When the ME Super is on AUTO the exposure compensation dial *must* be used for sequences of bracketed shots – photographers who are accustomed to using a manual only camera and bracketing with the aperture ring should note this well. Normally exposures at $\frac{1}{2}\times$, $1\times$ and $2\times$ will be adequate to yield one satisfactory photograph, but for additional cover you could use the whole range between $\frac{1}{4}\times$ and $4\times$. Control is stepless throughout this range, so intermediate values can be set.

Underexposure can be used as a technique to darken the entire subject, and may give a nocturnal or – as in this case – macabre impression. It takes a good photographic eye to recognize suitable subjects.

Overexposure often makes for a high key effect which can be flattering in portraits of women. Colour tends to become washed out, however, so it is worth experimenting carefully with the technique.

General observations

A good deal of space has been devoted here to the subject of exposure compensation. This is because it is a very important link in the chain of controls that leads to the final image. Having learned to disregard erroneous meter readings based on information that, though factually correct, is either surplus to the requirements of the photograph or ambiguous because it fails to take into account the reflective qualities of the subject, the photographer will be in a position to decide whether his picture is to be a record or an interpretation. If a record, there is not much latitude for varying the exposure either way from the correct level. If an interpretation, exposure is of course only one of the factors that can be manipulated.

If negative films are being used the final image can be extensively worked on at the printing stage, and although mistakes cannot necessarily be fully eradicated they can often be skilfully masked. (This is not intended to imply that skilled printing consists solely of hiding exposure errors.) There is no second chance with transparencies, however; the exposure *must* be correct, and therefore this is the most demanding branch of photography. These observations on exposure compensation apply principally to photographers who work with reversal films.

The following table lists some situations in which the use of exposure factors should at least be considered. It would not be constructive to suggest exactly what the factor should be in each case because relative luminosity varies so widely. The table clearly cannot be comprehensive. It may be instructive, but, as always, a description of the mouldings is no substitute for possession of the matrix.

Increase exposure

$1 \times \longrightarrow 2 \times \longrightarrow 4 \times$

Portraits or still lifes against the sky or against a window
Subjects with strong directional backlighting
Landscapes under a clear sky
Snow scenes
Misty scenes
When thin diluted colours are required
When it is important to retain detail in shadow areas of contrasty subjects
Whitewashed buildings, expanses of glass and concrete
When high key effects are sought
Any other subject that is predominantly white or pale in colour

Reduce exposure

$\frac{1}{4} \times \longleftarrow \frac{1}{2} \times \longleftarrow 1 \times$

City lights at night
Stained glass in dark buildings
Subjects with a dark framework, e.g. outdoor scenes framed by doors, windows or branches
Telephoto pictures of the moon
Rainbows
Silhouette effects
Sunsets
When it is important to retain detail in highlight areas of contrasty subjects
Subjects picked out by spotlighting, e.g. on stage
When low key or nocturnal effects are sought
When strong and saturated colours are sought
Any other subject that is predominantly black or dark in colour

8 The ME Super on Manual

For all that automation has opened up new horizons in photography, particularly where the photographer is striving to remain alert and vigilant in the rough and tumble of the human maelstrom, there are still situations in which automatic control is inappropriate; there are also borderline cases where personal preference dictates which mode is the more suitable. What cannot be disputed is that no automatic system can claim to be complete unless it can be switched off, leaving the photographer in charge of all operations, with the option of using the TTL meter if he wishes.

The status of manual exposure control as an equal partner in more advanced photography is reflected in the concern of the ME Super designers to re-examine the *whole* of the traditional concept of camera logistics. The result is not just last year's manual camera with a silicon chip on its shoulder. The manual system developed for the ME Super is itself revolutionary, an application of micro-electronics to a previously unmodernized area of camera manufacture, and is fully integrated with the electronic shutter control mechanism and viewfinder LED display.

Preparing the camera for manual exposure

The exposure mode selection dial is turned to M; film speed should be set and the exposure compensation dial set to 1 × as for automatic exposure.

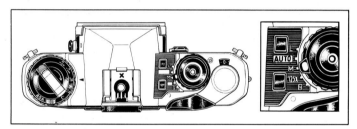

Setting shutter speed

This is performed completely by touch, with the eye to the viewfinder.

Light pressure on the shutter release button illuminates the LED display in the viewfinder for about 30 seconds, in the same way as for automatic exposure. The green M LED second from the top will glow continuously, confirming that the ME Super is set in its manual mode.

One of the shutter speed LEDs will be illuminated. This will always be the shutter speed that was last set, because the manual system is equipped with a memory that survives *everything* except removal or expiry of the batteries. Thus, if a shutter speed of 2 secs has been set, you can take a sequence of shots on AUTO and/or 125× and/or B, change films and ASA ratings as often as you like, fit and remove flash units, motor winders various lenses etc., and leave the camera unused in a cupboard for six months; but next time it is switched to the M setting the 2S LED will glow.

Shutter speed is altered not by the conventional dial with click-stops but electromechanically by either of the two rectangular black buttons located between the exposure mode selector and the pentaprism housing. A key feature of these buttons is that they are within easy reach of the finger resting on the shutter button. Either of them is touch-located without hesitation, so that the camera need not be taken from the eye. They respond to the lightest of touches, which gives the action an unprecedented smoothness.

To increase shutter speed: press the button toward the front of the camera. Shutter speed will increase, stepping smoothly from one LED to the next one up until the finger is removed from the button. The LED that is lit at the moment the finger is lifted will remain lit, and denotes the speed that is set.

To reduce shutter speed: press the button toward the back of the camera. The LEDs are illuminated serially in descending order from faster to slower shutter speeds. Either process is far more efficient than turning a dial.

Setting a particular speed is, of course, simply a matter of lifting the finger from the button when the relevant LED is illuminated. If you should overshoot, returning a step or two is very easy: a quick touch on either button, without maintaining the pressure, alters shutter speed by one step.

In either direction, when the end of the scale is reached it starts again at the beginning. That is, if you are pressing the front 'increase' button, the LEDs will light successively up to 2000, then, without pausing, revert to 4S and begin climbing again. In the other direction the jump is from 4S to 2000, then on down the scale again. Either button alone is obviously sufficient to enable any speed to be chosen; two are provided to make small adjustments between adjacent settings as quick and easy as possible. For adjustments between the extremes of the scale, rather than climb through it in the regular fashion, it is quicker to go off at one end as the sequence immediately recommences at the other.

Exposure metering

When the camera is set in its manual mode the exposure information from aperture and shutter speed controls is still linked to, and co-ordinated by, the light meter. Subject to the conditions outlined in the previous chapter (pages 68-71) exposure will be correct when neither the red UNDER nor the OVER LED is flashing. (When activated, these LEDs flash on manual but glow continuously on AUTO—see page 54. Note also that it is relatively uncommon for either of the LEDs to light up on AUTO, because there is usually an automatic shutter speed that will match the aperture selected. However, on manual one or the other of them will flash constantly until aperture and shutter speed match for correct exposure.)

Setting the ME Super manually consists of adjusting either aperture or shutter speed, or both, until neither the UNDER nor the OVER LED is flashing in the viewfinder. This operation is very quick to perform.

Exposure compensation

When the ME Super is being used in its manual mode, the 'correct' exposure indicated by the absence of flashing OVER or UNDER LEDs will be *identical* to the automatically 'correct' exposure indicated with the camera on AUTO. If you establish correct exposure on manual and then switch over to AUTO without moving the camera from the subject, all that will happen is that the green M LED will go out: apart from that there will be no change, the same shutter speed LED remaining lit. So far as the response of the light meter is concerned, it makes no difference whether the camera is on AUTO or M: the choice is there solely for the convenience of the user. It will be obvious, therefore, that in all the situations outlined on pages 68-71, the same comments about overriding the meter will apply.

However, on manual the operation can be carried out in three different ways: (i) by adjusting the exposure compensation dial; (ii) by varying the aperture, and (iii) by varying the shutter speed. Options (ii) and (iii) will be familiar to anyone who is accustomed to using a manual-only camera.

Adjusting the exposure compensation dial
The procedure is the same whether the ME Super is set to M or AUTO (see page 70), but the effect is different. On M, the exposure compensation dial does not affect the shutter speed: it reprogrammes the meter so that either the OVER or the UNDER LED will direct the camera user to a different

When photographing against a bright background you will find it necessary to take an exposure meter reading from the subject alone. In this example the right-hand picture was exposed according to a reading taken from the mail box, while the one on the left was taken on AUTO. The difference was a surprising six stops. This is outside the range of the exposure compensation dial, so the manual mode must be used.

exposure. For example: with the dial at 1× exposure is correct at, say f/8 at 1/250 sec. Alter the dial to ½× and the OVER LED will begin to flash, and will continue to do so until either the aperture is reset to f/11 or shutter speed to 1/500. Alter the dial to ¼× instead and the OVER LED will flash until *either* the aperture is reset to f/16, *or* the shutter speed is reset to 1/1000, *or* both aperture and shutter speed are reset to f/11 and 1/500 respectively. At the same time the red EF LED will flash until the dial is reset to 1×, as on AUTO.

Exposure compensation by aperture or shutter speed

Experienced photographers working in the manual mode may prefer to bypass the exposure compensation dial. Having established 'correct' exposure as a guide, you can alter either aperture or shutter speed entirely at your discretion, disregarding the OVER or UNDER LED. This is the only method that can be used when exposure factors of more than 2× and ¼× are to be employed.

Exposure compensation is one of the principal functions of manual control. Although two stops either way will be sufficient for the majority of situations, there remain occasions when the adventurous photographer will need greater flexibility. Manual override provides this.

Additionally, bracketing exposures is equally easy on manual, and can be done either by altering the aperture or the shutter speed (but not the exposure compensation dial). To bracket exposures by aperture, start at one extremity of your chosen range and turn the aperture ring as you advance the film after each exposure: each click-stop of the ring represents a half stop increase or decrease in exposure. Bracketing by shutter speed is hardly slower: shoot—advance film—press the shutter speed button lightly once—shoot—etc. Most users find the forward button marginally easier to locate when speed is all-important, so start the bracketed sequence at a speed *slower* than the metered setting.

When to use the manual mode

The main uses of the manual mode are in low-light photography in which long exposures may be necessary, for studies of moving subjects in which it is essential to have absolute control over shutter speed, and, as described above, for situations where the automatic mode is not flexible enough to cater for extremes or anomalies of subject lighting. For some people manual is the standard mode, automation providing a back-up mode for use in unfamiliar situations or when perhaps a friend is borrowing the camera for the day.

Manual speed selection is invaluable for fine control in sport and action photography. If fast movement is to be 'frozen' by the use of a fast shutter speed, or if motion-blur effects are wanted, necessitating a relatively long exposure, the photographer needs to know that the speed he has selected will not be varied by any electronic brain. Care must then be taken with exposure: panning a fast-moving object that moves from sun into shade or vice versa, as can easily happen in partially enclosed places such as sports grounds, could lead to badly washed out or impenetrably dense photographs if the automatic function is not ready and waiting to make ultra-fast adjustments at a moment's notice.

Fog at night – the B setting is useful for nocturnal shooting.

Time exposures on 'B'

When the exposure mode selection dial is at B the shutter will remain open for as long as the release button is kept depressed. The camera must be mounted on a tripod and a cable release should be screwed into the hole in the shutter release button—finger pressure applied directly to the camera is likely to cause slight vibration. Most cable releases are fitted with a locking device, which is useful for exposures of longer than a few seconds.

Metering in dim light can be a problem. Outside the coupling range of the meter it is possible to get a reading by increasing the ASA number on the camera and working backwards, always bearing in mind that accuracy is not guaranteed. Open up to maximum aperture and, with the camera on manual, set the shutter speed to 4S. Activate the meter: if the UNDER LED is flashing, increase the film speed setting by doubling the ASA rating one or more times. A reading will result sooner or later, except in almost total blackness, and from this you can work backwards to the required exposure as follows:

For each time the ASA number is halved in getting the film speed dial back to the actual rating of the film in use, double the exposure time.

For each stop you close the aperture down from the setting at which the meter reading was established, double the exposure time.

If using colour film, double the result twice more to compensate for the effects of reciprocity failure.

Bracket the exposures. This means doubling up again at least once, but it increases the chance of obtaining one good result.

All this doubling can result in some very long exposures indeed, and the results may sometimes be disappointing, although at best they can be really spectacular. In many cases of night-time exposures, however, the purpose is not necessarily to simulate daylight, which is what the above method is designed to do. More often the darkness forms a backdrop for patterns of moving or stationary coloured lights. Fireworks, fairground lights, car head and tail lights and lightning flashes are examples of this type of subject. To record these the shutter can be held open for up to about 30 seconds or so at f/11, until you judge that enough lines, streaks or points have been stored up on a single piece of emulsion to make an interesting photograph.

9 Filters

Many light sources do not emit radiation of all visible wavelengths in equal measure—in other words, they are some colour other than white (see page 10). Unless an object is illuminated by white light, its colours are inaccurately rendered in photography. They are in everyday life as well, but we do not notice that.

Colour reversal emulsions are therefore balanced to give natural-*seeming* colour reproduction in the kind of conditions typically encountered by photographers, namely, daylight from the sun and sky and tungsten light from electric bulbs, the former having an exaggerated blue and the latter an exaggerated red component. If exposed to pure white light under laboratory conditions, daylight-type film would have a slight pinkish cast and tungsten films an unmistakable blue one because of this built-in colour compensation factor. Fortunately we do not live under laboratory conditions and the normal films meet our expectations very well.

But there are many occasions when the colour quality of the light source departs slightly or drastically from that for which the film in the camera is balanced. Since the eye is so insensitive to such changes until it sees them in photographs, it is a good idea to develop a suspicious attitude towards light sources in general and ask yourself regularly not *whether* a filter is necessary, but *what* filter is necessary. Only rarely are filters entirely superfluous.

In black and white photography an orange or red filter can be used to darken the sky without darkening the clouds. Skies are often uninteresting if no filter is used.

Gelatin Filter Holder

The Pentax Gelatin Filter Holder is available in four sizes (49, 52, 58 and 77mm) and enables a single 3-inch square Kodak or other gelatin filter to be used on lenses of different sizes, so that it is not necessary to buy one of each filter for each lens. The holder is very easy to use; it can be adapted to hold more than one filter, clips on simply and securely to the front of the lens, and can be rotated.

Lens Hoods

If bright light is allowed to fall directly on to the lens, even if its source is outside the picture area it can cause flare, reducing contrast and colour saturation and even causing colours to alter. Lens hoods are designed to box off the lens from extraneous light. In doing this they also afford the delicate glass some protection against accidental handling and help to keep out rain, spray, dust and dirt.

All SMC Pentax lenses except the most extreme wide-angles can be fitted with a lens hood. A flexible type is also available and is a good choice when arduous working conditions are anticipated and extra robustness is required.

A landscape taken on infra-red film. Blue sky comes out black, and it is grass, not sand, on the ground. A deep red filter must be used with monochrome infra-red film.

Colour-correction filter chart

Filter name	Light source	Effect	Availability (mm)
Skylight	Skylight, i.e. not in direct sun	Absorbs excessive blue in scenes lit by skylight alone; particularly valuable in landscape photography	49, 52, 58, 67, 77 (standard) 49, 52, 58, 67, 77 (SMC)
Cloudy	Daylight	Absorbs excess blue in outdoor work under a cloudy sky	49, 52 (standard) 49, 52, 58, 67, 77 (SMC)
Morning and Evening	Early and late sun	Reduces the excess orange-red of the rising or setting sun. Should not be used if the sunrise or sunset is itself the subject of the picture	49, 52 (standard)
Flash	Clear flash bulbs	Must be used with clear flash bulbs (not electronic flash)	49, 52 (standard)
Flood	Photofloods	Makes possible the use of daylight film with photo-flood lighting; also with general service domestic bulbs	49, 52 (standard)
FLR	Fluorescent tubes	Counteracts the unpleasant greenish tints obtained with daylight film under fluorescent lighting	49, 52 (standard)
Polarizing	Daylight	Cuts down surface reflections on glass and water; intensifies the blue of the sky	49, 52, 58 (standard)
UV	Daylight	SMC Pentax lenses are in any case opaque to ultra-violet light and do not need this filter. However, it makes a useful permanent lens protector	49, 52, 58, 67, 77 (standard) 49, 52, 58, 67, 77 (SMC)

N.B. SMC Pentax filters are treated with the same 7-layer coating of rare elements as the SMC lenses; this improves light transmission and hence sharpness and contrast (see page 122)

Filters for use with black and white film

Name	Colour	Effect	Availability (mm)
Y1	Pale yellow	Absorbs a small amount of blue light, and thus darkens the sky slightly so that white clouds become more prominent	49, 52 (standard)
Y2	Medium yellow	Similar to but stronger than Y1; especially valuable in landscape photography	49, 52, 58, 67, 77 (standard) 49, 52, 58, 67, 77 (SMC)
O2	Orange	Increases cloud-sky contrast more than yellow filters; also improves surface texture of brick and stone	49, 52, 58, 67, 77 (standard) 49, 52, 58, 67, 77 (SMC)
R2	Red	Similar to orange but stronger: makes sky almost black. R2 must be used with black and white infra-red film	49, 52 (standard) 49, 52, 58, 67, 77 (SMC)
YG	Yellow-green	Darkens red and lightens green. Improves skin tones and is therefore especially useful for outdoor portraits	49, 52 (standard)

Polarizing—Effect and availability as for colour film.

Special effects filters

Fantastic colour filters (all available in 49 and 52mm sizes)

Name	Effect
R/B	Filter changes from blue to red then back to blue as it is rotated; can be stopped at any intermediate stage
R/G	As for R/B, but colour changing from red through amber to green

Magic image attachments (for both colour and black and white film)

Name	Effect
5C	A prism filter which divides the image into six, the central area being repeated in the outer five facets
4C	The same as the above, but with four facets surrounding the central one
2C	The same as the above, but with two facets situated either side of the central one
6M	One half of the picture area is normal, the other consists of the central part of the image repeated in five vertical bars
CF	Central focusing: the centre of the image is sharp while a romantic softness is introduced at the edges; very flattering in portraiture

People

1. The use of a polarizing filter has increased colour saturation, but it is above all the viewpoint that makes this arresting and atmospheric composition

2–3. Two examples of shutter blur adding a sense of movement to pictures of people

4. The string trio, posed formally in a suitable setting, have about them an air of authority

5. An informally posed group of workmen from a Portuguese wine-growing village

6. The great Kenyan athlete Kip Keino is the prominent figure in the group taken with a telephoto lens

7. A marvellous overhead view of an old western ritual: the bookmaker handing out money to a lucky—or shrewd—punter

8. Zulu dancers kicking up clouds of dust, almost obscuring the drummers in the background

1. Schoolchildren, Nairobi, Kenya

2. Red China

3. Bangladesh

4. Dorchester Cathedral

5. Portugal

6. Kenya

7. England

8. South Africa

Children

1. Despite the evident high spirits of the children the photographer has taken care to make use of the entire picture area

2. Notice the camera position—not looking down at the child, but straight at him: always a point worth remembering

3. Expose for the highlights to get a good dark background

4. Depth of field is shallow at close range: focusing on the child's hand increases the mild humour of a shot like this

5. A semi-formal portrait of a child: her face is lit by a white reflector, not direct sun

6. This child's attention is engaged by another person, standing behind and above the photographer; such assistance often helps with younger subjects

7. The sun is at just the right angle to give edge-lighting to the figure and a vivid glow to the balloons

8. The photographer has prefocused the camera and exposed for the highlights for this spontaneous-seeming picture

Children 1

Children 2

Children 3

Children 4

Children 5

Children 6

Children 7

Children 8

Sport

1. Spectacular effect achieved by fixing the camera (fitted with a fish-eye lens) to the wing of the hang glider

2. The barren landscape of New Mexico provides an almost monochromatic background for the brightly coloured hot air balloon

3. Action photography in low light—a slow shutter speed, vertical panning and the use of high-speed Ektachrome are combined in this shot of the Rumanian tennis star Virginia Ruzici

4—5. Two interpretations of team sport—a fast shutter speed freezes the American footballers against the shaded spectators, while a slow shutter blurs the movement of the association footballers

6—9. Moments of stillness and tension convey a sense of the sportsman's tight control over his own strength

10—13. Immaculate camera technique and a dynamic sense of composition contribute to the sense of speed and action in these masterful and impressionistic sporting photographs.

1. Hang glider

2. Albuquerque, New Mexico

3. Virginia Ruzici

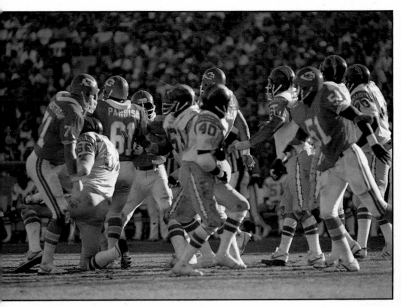

4. San Diego *vs* Kansas City

5. Association football

6. Jack Nicklaus at Palm Springs

7. Moscow Olympics, 1980

8. Moscow Olympics, 1980

9. 100 metres sprint

10. Hans Klemmer of Austria

11. Diamond Head, Hawaii

12. The Grand National, Aintree

13. Brands Hatch

Fashion and glamour

1. A close-framed shot such as this can be taken almost anywhere as there is virtually no background

2. Avoiding eye-contact with the viewer gives the model a demure and retiring appearance

3. Model lit by diffused flash from the right of the picture—the candles are purely decorative

4. The highly reflective background suppresses shadows and contributes an aggressive glare to this fashion shot

5. A soft-focus attachment softens the outlines of a 'sculptural' nude; the lighting is warm and low key

6. Shooting against hard sunlight can impart graphic strength to nudes on the beach, without destroying the sensuousness of the female form

7. The girl looks relaxed and at ease—awkward posing spoils photographs even if the model is attractive

Fashion and glamour 1

Fashion and glamour 2

Fashion and glamour 3

Fashion and glamour 4

Fashion and glamour 5

Fashion and glamour 6

Fashion and glamour 7

Portraits

1. A composition of uncommon strength, for which no elaborate props or equipment were needed—only the right pose

2. An atmospheric portrait of jazz pianist Oscar Peterson

3. The sun was at just the right angle for this portrait of a Mediterranean woman, but the photographer had to take a meter reading from the highlights to get the exposure right

4. A posed but informal outdoor portrait

5. Electronic flash has been used to supplement daylight—you can see the reflections of both in the eyes

6. How much of your subject should you include in a portrait? Singer Phil Lynott's posture is as eloquent as his facial expression

7. His Grace the Duke of Beaufort at home: sepia toning of black and white prints is appropriate to some subjects

8. Slight underexposure was necessary to preserve the natural skin tones in this portrait of an unusual subject

Portraits 1

Portraits 2: Oscar Peterson

Portraits 3

Portraits 4

Portraits 5

Portraits 6: Phil Lynott of Thin Lizzy

Portraits 7: The Duke of Beaufort

Portraits 8

10 Electronic flash with the Pentax ME Super

Electronic flash units provide a lightweight but extremely efficient form of artificial lighting. They have a re-usable gas-filled tube in place of the disposable bulbs that were familiar until quite recently, and this makes them very economical to run, despite a relatively high initial cost. One tube will give thousands of flashes; the only parts that need replacement are the batteries, and with the energy-saving thyristor circuitry incorporated into today's more sophisticated units wastage of battery power has been virtually eliminated.

If a flash unit is of the so-called 'dedicated' type this means that it has been designed specifically for use with a particular camera or range of cameras. In the case of Pentax dedicated-type flash units the compatibility takes the form of electronic links between the viewfinder LED display of the ME Super (also the ME-F, LX and MG) and the switching and charging components of the flash units. Normally the user has to set the shutter speed on the camera manually and check a neon indicator on the unit itself in order to establish when it is ready to fire. Relaying the information into the viewfinder cuts out this stage and enables the photographer to keep his eye on the subject without interruption. Furthermore, while the unit is charging or recycling, or switched off, it ceases to override the automatic (or manual) shutter speed; therefore there is no moment at which the camera is out of action—available light can always be used as a stop-gap.

How it works

The following sequence describes the use of a Pentax dedicated-type flash unit with the ME Super.

(i) The unit is attached to the hot shoe of the ME Super (or to a bracket mount in the case of the AF 400-T), the film speed set and a power output selected as directed, and switched on. A current begins to flow from the batteries to the capacitor (a device which stores the charge, which is too weak to fire the tube when it comes direct from the batteries).

(ii) When the capacitor has stored enough electrical energy to fire the flash tube, the green M LED begins to flash on and off in the viewfinder; simultaneously the green 125× LED lights up to indicate that the opening of the shutter and firing of the flash will be synchronized.

(iii) The photographer makes the exposure. As the shutter opens the flash circuit is closed and the capacitor discharges into the gas-filled tube, which begins to emit a strong beam of light.

(iv) Light reflected from the subject is monitored or 'computed' by a sensor on the flash unit. When the amount of light received by the sensor reaches a preset level determined by film speed, the current from capacitor to flash tube is interrupted by an electronic switching component called a thyristor, and the beam of light is switched off. It may have lasted only 1/30000 sec or so, although often more.

(v) The capacitor begins to recharge. If the flash was a brief one, very little charge will have been expended and the recycling will only take a second or two. Recycling time is longer after a more prolonged flash. In the mean time the M and 125× LEDs are extinguished and the viewfinder display reverts to its previous state, whichever mode it was set in. It also reverts as soon as the flash unit is switched off or removed.

With dedicated-type flash units the whole operation is simple and efficient. Nevertheless, the ME Super has facilities for the connection of any electronic flash unit, including those requiring a cord socket.

Operating instructions

Pentax dedicated-type flash units (AUTO operation)

The ME Super should be set to either its AUTO or M mode and the flash unit fitted into the hot shoe on top of the pentaprism housing (except for the AF-400T, which is carried on a bracket mount and connected by a cord plugged into the X-synch socket of the camera).

Set the film speed (not necessary on the AF 160) and switch the unit on. Until the capacitor is fully charged the camera remains operational without flash. All Pentax electronic flash units, and many other types, have a choice of power settings: more distant subjects or slow films necessitate the use of a high setting (red band), while the low setting (green band) is for use with faster films and closer subjects. There is a broad area of overlap, in which the use of the green setting helps to conserve battery life. By reference to the colour-coded scale printed on the back of the flash unit, work out the correct f/number and set the aperture ring on the camera accordingly.

In some places photography would quite simply be impossible without flash.

Focus the lens, making sure that the subject is within the area of coverage for the power output you have selected. If it is not, the light reaching the subject will be either too weak or too intense for correct exposure.

Make the exposure as soon as possible after the LED display has indicated that everything is ready. Switch the unit off at once unless you intend to make more exposures by flash. There is no need to remove it from the camera if you wish to have it ready for use at a moment's notice.

Other electronic flash units

An electronic flash unit made by an independent manufacturer will work as well with Pentax SLRs as with any other camera. There is no disadvantage to using them except that you lose the convenience and the extras that go with dedicated units.

Set the exposure mode dial of the ME Super to 125×. As the exposure is controlled by correct setting of lens aperture and flash unit, the design of which may differ from Pentax units, there is no viewfinder LED display in the 125× mode.

From this point on, follow the instructions supplied by the manufacturer of the flash unit. As exposure is then entirely dependent on correct functioning of the unit, the role of the ME Super is reduced to one of synchronization. Should the results obtained be disappointing, the fault is almost certain to lie in the flash unit and not in the ME Super.

Manual operation: the guide number system

All Pentax electronic flash units and most other types have at least one manual setting for use in certain problematic situations. When a flash unit is set on manual the thyristor is bypassed and the full charge of the capacitor or a measured proportion of it is spent with each flash, exposure being regulated by choice of aperture rather than flash duration. As the maximum power rating of flash units varies, each one is given a 'guide number' or a scale of guide numbers enabling the user to work out the correct aperture on the basis of film speed and flash-to-subject distance. Where a single guide number is given, this refers to film rated at 100 ASA, with distances in metric. Sometimes imperial conversions are also given.

To work out the correct f/number, divide the guide number by the flash-to-subject distance—it is as simple as that.

The manual procedure involves resetting the aperture for each exposure, whereas with computerized operation exposure control is automated within the chosen range and all the user has to do is focus. Thyristor circuitry also has the advantage of being economical of battery power.

However, manual control offers advantages which in some situations cannot be overlooked. The essential difference is that on manual, the amount of light that is *delivered* is fixed while that received back into the camera is variable according to subject qualities; on automatic the amount of light *received* at the camera position is fixed, the quantity delivered being the variable factor. The drawbacks of automatic exposure control with subjects that are not typical have been described on pages 68-71. The same principles apply with automatic flash: subjects which are predominantly either very light or very dark, or subjects of average tone set against dark or light backgrounds, will tend to be incorrectly rendered by the automatic process.

Pentax electronic flash units

Pentax AF 160

Guide no.	ASA	25	64	80	100	125	200	400	800
	metres	8	13	14	16	18	22	32	44
	feet	24	39	42	48	54	66	96	132

Auto modes	Red (high); green (low)
Auto flash range	Red: 1-6m (3-20ft) Green: 0.5-4m (3-20ft)
Manual operation	'M' setting of Auto/Manual selector

Maximum range at f/2 (Manual)	ASA	25	64	80	100	125	200	400	800
	metres	4	6.5	7	8	9	11	16	22
	feet	12	19	21	24	27	33	48	66

Approximate recycling time and no. of flashes	With alkaline batteries: 8 sec, 200 flashes With manganese batteries: 10 sec, 40 flashes Recycling time varies with power source, state of batteries and duration of previous flash
Angular spread	50° vertical, 65° horizontal—compatible with lenses between 28mm wide-angle and 50mm standard
Other features	Flash ready lamp on unit, information relayed to viewfinder with ME Super, ME-F and MG; TEST flash button; colour-coded exposure information chart on back

Pentax AF 200S

Guide no.	ASA	25	64	80	100	125	200	400	800
	metres	10	16	18	20	22	28	40	56
	feet	30	48	54	60	66	84	120	168

Auto modes	Red (high); green (low)
Auto flash range	Red: 1.4-7.1m (4½-23½ft) Green: 0.6-3.5m (2-11½ft)
Manual operation	'MAN' setting of Auto/Manual selector

Maximum range at f/2 (Manual)	ASA	25	64	80	100	125	200	400	800
	metres	5	8	9	10	11	14	20	28
	feet	15	24	27	30	33	42	60	84

Approximate recycling time and no. of flashes	With alkaline batteries: 6 sec, 250 flashes With manganese batteries: 8 sec, 60 flashes Recycling time varies with power source, state of batteries and duration of previous flash
Angular spread	50° vertical, 65° horizontal—compatible with lenses between 28mm wide-angle and 50mm standard without optional adaptors
Other features	Flash ready lamp on unit, information relayed to viewfinder with ME Super, ME-F and MG; Test flash button; colour-coded exposure information by sliding scale on back of unit. Supplied with case. Optional extras: AFW1 wide-angle adaptor (down to 24mm wide-angle); AFT1 Tele Lens Adaptor (up to 135mm telephoto)

Pentax AF 280T

Guide no.	ASA	25	64	80	**100**	125	200	400	800
	metres	14	22	25	**28**	31	40	55	80
	feet	42	66	75	**84**	93	120	165	240

Auto modes	Three: TTL (for LX); red (high); green (low)
Non-TTL auto flash range	Red: 1-7m (3½-24ft) Green: 0.5-3.5m (1½-12ft)
Manual operation	Three settings: High/Low with auto synch for ME Super, MG, ME-F and LX; full manual override

Maximum range at f/2 (manual)	ASA	25	64	80	**100**	125	200	400	800
	metres	7	11	12.5	**14**	15.5	20	28	40
	feet	21	33	38	**42**	47	60	84	120

Approximate recycling time	0.5-10 sec, depending on state of batteries and duration of previous flash
No. of flashes	up to 550+
Bounce capability	Head rotates full 180° horizontally and 105° vertically, both with click-stops; sensor remains pointed at subject
Other features	Flash ready lamp on unit, information relayed to viewfinder with ME Super, ME-F and MG; Auto check lamp; provision for TTL flash metering with LX; 6-way flash mode selector; colour coded exposure information scales; TEST flash button. Supplied with case

Pentax AF 400T

Guide no.	ASA	25	64	80	**100**	125	200	400	800
	metres	20	32	35	**40**	44	56	80	112
	feet	60	96	105	**120**	132	168	240	336

Auto modes	Four: TTL (for Pentax LX), red, green and yellow
Non-TTL auto flash range	Red: 0.45-10m (1½-30ft) Green: 0.45-5m (1½-15ft) Yellow: 0.45-3.5m (1½-12ft)
Manual operation	Five settings: Full, 1/2, 1/4, 1/8 with auto synch for ME Super, ME-F, LX and MG; full manual override

Maximum range at f/2 (manual)	ASA	25	64	80	**100**	125	200	400	800
	metres	10	16	17	**20**	22	28	40	64
	feet	30	48	51	**60**	66	84	120	192

Approximate recycling time	0.2-12 sec, depending on state of power source and on duration of previous flash
No. of flashes	up to 800+
Bounce capability	Head rotates full 180° horizontally and 105° vertically, both with click-stops; sensor remains pointed at subject
Other features	Optional extras include bracket mount; synch cord 4P; NiCad battery case; Multi-flash cord; Grip Battery Pack; TR Power pack; 510-volt High Voltage Power Pack; 270v/240v High Voltage Power Pack; AC Adaptor

Techniques of flash photography

The nature of flash light

To make the best use of an electronic flash unit, whether or not it is of the dedicated type, it is important to be familiar with the nature and composition of the light that it produces. However intense the light may be when first generated, coming from a relatively small source it loses in intensity rapidly as it spreads out, covering a wider and wider area with increasing distance. In fact, brightness falls off with the square of the distance from flash to subject, which means that at any given distance its intensity will be only one-quarter of that at half the distance; e.g. an object at 10 metres from the camera will require an exposure four times as great as an object 5 metres from the camera, and this in turn will require an exposure four times as great as an object 2.5 metres from the camera (by application of a law of physics known as the *inverse square law*). So although it looks and is very bright at source, the light from a flash unit of average power is only useful at short and medium range.

Flash light is also highly directional. This means that when it is fixed to the hot shoe of a camera it emits a harsh frontal light that can be crude and unsubtle in some contexts, flattening contours, highlighting reflective surfaces and drawing dense black lines of shadow below objects that are too close to their background. Foreground objects can stand out brilliantly against large areas of deep shadow—very effective at certain times, but artificial-seeming at others.

The colour of electronic flash light is similar to that of noon daylight. This means that daylight-type colour reversal films can be used without filtration when a neutral result is required. It is worth remembering that where flash is used to swamp other artificial light sources its light may appear to be rather cold and clinical in quality, and the use of a pale amber filter sometimes helps to restore the atmosphere of the original scene.

Electronic flash casts a brilliant and rather clinical light that freezes movement and throws hard shadows behind the subject if it is close to a background.

Use flash in the manual mode for a black background (left) and in either mode when using more than one unit (right).

Bounced flash

The flash head of the Pentax AF 280T and the AF 400T can be pivoted vertically or horizontally while the sensor, being mounted in the body of the unit, remains in a fixed forward-pointing position to monitor the light reflected back from the subject. If the flash head is pointed towards a suitable surface, rather than directly at the subject, the illumination will appear to originate from that surface rather than from the flash unit. The hard, contour-levelling effect of direct camera-mounted flash is avoided in this way, and if the reflecting surface is matt rather than polished it will also act as a diffuser. The result is that a more natural-looking light is cast on the subject, while the sensor ensures that the duration of the flash is regulated to compensate by exactly the right amount for the loss of intensity caused by the extra distance that the light has to travel. Directing the flash towards the ceiling simulates soft skylight, while if it is bounced off a wall the effect is more like window light.

There are two notable pitfalls: if the surface used as a reflector/diffuser is coloured the effect will be of a coloured light source, which may be inappropriate or disagreeable; and if it is dark it may not reflect enough light to make the exposure. A matt or eggshell painted surface in off-white to cream is ideal. The reflecting surface should not appear in the picture, but on the other hand if it is too far away the subject may effectively be beyond the flash range, because the *total* flash-to-subject distance has to be taken into account when the power output is selected. The telephoto lens adaptor may help to overcome this problem if the subject cannot easily be moved; it is not essential to use a telephoto lens in this instance.

The AF 160 and AF 200S units do not have the swivelling head but can still be used for bounced flash. It is necessary first to obtain an extension lead which fits between the foot of the unit and the hot shoe of the ME Super, so that the flash unit can be held in the hand and directed away from the subject. It *must* then be used in its manual mode, with lens aperture worked out from the guide number divided by the total flash-reflector-subject distance. It will also be necessary to open up a further two stops or so to compensate for light absorbed by the reflector—perhaps one stop will be enough if it is brilliant white, two or more if it is darker. If a surface could conceivably be called 'dark' it will almost certainly be useless for bounced flash unless covered by pale fabric or paper. A screen of the type used for projecting transparencies can be a useful mobile reflector.

Flash off the camera

An extension lead of the type described above can be used with any flash unit designed for hot shoe mounting, and cord extension cables are also available in various lengths. These make possible numerous different lighting effects using a single flash unit.

Flash units can be used off the camera in any position—above, below, in front of or behind the subject—but not actually within the picture area unless concealed behind some other object (which will then appear as a silhouette). For most purposes use one of the automatic modes exactly as if the flash unit were attached to the camera: the area where the light falls should then be correctly exposed. For special circumstances such as side-lighting portraits or semi-abstract landscapes against the night sky, set the flash unit to its manual mode and work out the lens aperture from the guide number divided by the flash-to-subject distance.

Two or more electronic flash units can be used at once to give greater control over contrast, to highlight the hair of a portrait subject by rim-lighting, or to illuminate the background (excellent results can sometimes be obtained by sticking coloured transparent paper to a flash head illuminating the background). One powerful unit should be used off the camera to provide the main subject lighting, while a smaller unit mounted on the hot shoe provides a softer 'fill-in' light and in portraiture adds a sparkle to the eyes of the sitter. The off-the-camera unit should be activated by a 'slave' unit—a light-sensitive cell that triggers a flash tube in synchronization with the camera-mounted unit (slave units cannot be relied on in daylight). Exposure should be calculated on the basis of the main light alone, and may be either automatic or manual.

Fill-in flash

It is suggested on pages 68-71 in the context of exposure compensation that in situations where the ambient light is very contrasty, it is necessary to expose for either the highlight or the shadow areas, according to where you want detail to be recorded. But there may be another alternative: if the subject is close enough to be within electronic flash range, and shutter speed can be reduced to 125× or slower by adjustment of the aperture, the shadows can be 'filled-in' with light so that detail is retained over the entire scene. Once again, the real problem lies not in the technique, which is simple enough in itself; it is in recognizing the danger of losing details in parts of the scene.

The Pentax AF 160 and AF 200S are effective for fill-in flash up to a distance of about 3m (10ft), the AF 280T up to 4m (13ft) and the 400T up to 6m (20ft).

Before attaching the flash unit take a normal overall exposure reading with the ME Super on manual to establish the correct aperture with the shutter speed at 125×. Switch the flash unit on and set to manual operation, then reduce lens aperture by 1-2 stops. As soon as the capacitor is charged the exposure can be made.

11 The Pentax range of interchangeable lenses

There are currently well over 40 different lenses in the SMC Pentax family, and new improved versions are being introduced all the time. This is perhaps the most rapidly changing area in camera design, and while lenses of new specifications are regularly released on to the market, research continues into ways to effect major improvements to the entire range. No list can therefore be regarded as definitive, but compatibility with Pentax camera bodies now and for the future can be taken for granted.

The avenues opened up by this enormous range of lenses are long and colourful, but before exploring them more methodically it will help to look in some detail at modern lens design.

Why lenses are so complex

Simple glass lenses have inherent faults and imperfections that make them unsuitable for use with modern cameras and fine-grain emulsions. However precise the grinding and polishing of a single-element lens, the image it projects is not consistently sharp over the entire picture area. The aberrations may take the form of overall softness due to variations in the angle of refraction at different points on its surface (spherical aberration); a comet-like stretching of shapes at the edges of the image (coma); an inability to focus both radial and concentric lines simultaneously at the edges of the frame (astigmatism); a rendering of the sides of a square with its centre on the optical axis as either convex or concave (aptly named barrel and pincushion distortion respectively); splitting of light into its component colours (chromatic aberration), or inability to focus both the edges and the centre of the image at the same time (field curvature). Any lens consisting of a single glass element suffers from all these defects at once, to a greater or lesser degree. Modern lenses are made up of a number of elements brought together in such a way that they are mutually correcting—a nice simple statement for a task of such appalling complexity. That it can be achieved at all is a tribute to the pioneers of lens design; that it can be economically achieved in lightweight lenses, especially those with variable focal lengths (zoom lenses), would have been beyond belief to our predecessors and has only been made possible by the use of computers to provide detailed optical performance data that would formerly have taken many years to gather.

Modern lenses may contain many separate elements.

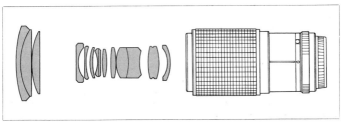

SMC: Super-Multi-Coating

The elements of compound lenses are made out of various types of glass with different refracting properties; but no matter what type of glass is used, each forward surface reflects some of the light that falls on it and transmits only what is left. This would not be too severe a handicap with single-element lenses, but it would render compound lenses very slow, and a lens with as many as fifteen elements would just not be conceivable.

Super-multi-coating is a 7-layer coating made up of rare elements that reduce the reflected component of light to an almost negligible quantity. It transmits light of all visible wavelengths uniformly, so that unlike the first generation of multi-coated lenses it is spectrally neutral and does not impart a colour cast to the final image; at the same time it is opaque to ultraviolet light and this obviates the need for a UV filter. The improved light transmission offered by SMC elements eliminates almost all of the internal reflections responsible for flare and ghost images.

Different lenses—what they do

The following descriptions cannot give a subjective impression of what different lenses do. If you are interested in lenses (and if you are interested in 35mm SLR photography you have to be interested in lenses) there is one certain way of finding out how they differ: go to a photo shop and look through a selection of them, moving the camera around as you do so. Seeing how the image changes as you pan and refocus lenses and substitute one for another has more impact than reading about their specifications and normal uses. But do read about them as well—lenses can be very seductive, capable of promising at a first encounter more than they can deliver in normal use.

Angle of view

The terms standard, wide-angle and telephoto are loosely used to designate most lenses, together with a set of figures when more precise information is required, e.g. '135mm f/3.5 telephoto'. All lenses reduce the three-dimensional world to a two-dimensional image and cut a disc out of it, which is then further masked by the rectangular film gate. The disc that a standard lens cuts out from the world appears in the viewfinder to be reproduced actual size—some photographers actually compose their shots with both eyes open, preferring their vision to be continuous rather than masked. A wide-angle lens cuts out a larger disc, but since it must form a standard-sized image the objects within it have to be reduced to fit. A telephoto lens has a narrow angle of view and extracts only a small disc, detail within which is correspondingly magnified so that it does not fall short of the image area. Viewing with both eyes open gives a good idea of the degree of reduction or magnification in these cases.

Focal length

The focal length of a lens is the distance in millimetres between the focal plane and the lens itself; in compound lenses the measurement is taken from a point at which the light paths from different parts of the subject cross over (remembering that the image at the film plane is inverted and laterally reversed). While there is often some coincidence between lenses of long focal lengths and lenses with large external dimensions, there is not a constant ratio.

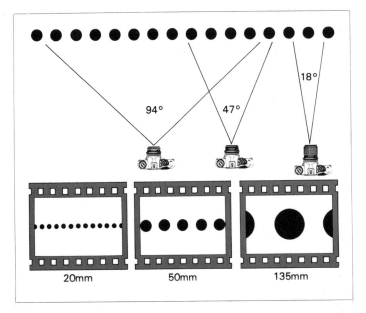

20mm   50mm   135mm

Diagram showing the difference to the picture of a theoretical subject when a wide-angle (left) or telephoto lens (right) is fitted in place of the standard lens.

A standard lens for a 35mm camera has a focal length of about 50mm. Lenses with a shorter focal length have a wider angle of view; those with a longer focal length have a narrower angle of view. The area scanned by a lens is inversely proportional to its focal length: if pointed at a large flat surface such as a wall, a 100mm lens will take in exactly half as much of it as a 50mm lens and twice as much as a 200mm lens, but of course, what it does take in will be reproduced at exactly twice or half of the size respectively on the film.

The focal length of a lens is engraved on the front of the barrel, together with another very important specification: its maximum aperture.

Maximum aperture or 'speed'

As explained on page 21, the iris diaphragm of a lens can be opened up or stopped down to regulate the flow of light through it. The widest diameter to which the diaphragm can be opened is known as the maximum aperture of the lens, and is expressed not as an absolute measurement but as a proportion of focal length. The numerical value (f/number) of any aperture is its diameter divided into the focal length of the lens. It is the f/number that is important, and not the diameter, because any given f/number transmits the same quantity of light whatever the focal length, whereas a given diameter does not. Once exposure values have been translated into any combination of aperture and shutter speed, they remain constant no matter what the focal length of the lens.

As examples, the maximum aperture of all the lenses in the diagram below left is f/2, but the actual diameter of the openings varies as shown. This is the reason for the existence of the universally accepted scale of f/numbers described on pages 21-22.

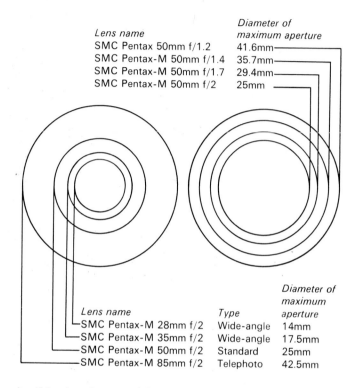

Lens name		Diameter of maximum aperture
SMC Pentax 50mm f/1.2		41.6mm
SMC Pentax-M 50mm f/1.4		35.7mm
SMC Pentax-M 50mm f/1.7		29.4mm
SMC Pentax-M 50mm f/2		25mm

Lens name	Type	Diameter of maximum aperture
SMC Pentax-M 28mm f/2	Wide-angle	14mm
SMC Pentax-M 35mm f/2	Wide-angle	17.5mm
SMC Pentax-M 50mm f/2	Standard	25mm
SMC Pentax-M 85mm f/2	Telephoto	42.5mm

It will be clear that as each increase of one f/stop doubles the area of the aperture, at the lower end of the scale the difference in absolute size is very large. Take for example the four 50mm standard lenses in the SMC Pentax range, with maximum apertures of f/1.2, f/1.4, f/1.7 and f/2, the actual sizes of which are shown above right.

The problem facing lens manufacturers is obviously not making iris diaphragms to these sizes—it is the grinding and polishing of the lens elements that have to double in size with each gain of one extra stop. The optical quality has to be maintained right up to the perimeter of the glass, otherwise there is no point in adding the extra stop at all: this is why lenses of identical focal lengths but different maximum apertures must vary so greatly in price (there is something very suspicious about it if they do not); it also accounts for the inclusion in the Pentax range of more than one lens of the most widely used focal lengths.

The term 'lens speed' is sometimes encountered, and lenses may be described as 'fast': this is simply a way of referring to lenses the maximum aperture of which is considered to be relatively large.

Special characteristics

Some lenses are designed for specialized branches of photography. See the individual descriptions of the following Pentax SMC lenses: Fish-eye 17mm f/4; Reflex 1000mm f/11; Reflex 2000mm f/13.5; Macro 50mm f/4; Macro 100mm f/4; Bellows 100mm f/4, and Shift 28mm f/3.5.

Situations in which it is essential to be able to change lenses: (above) the wildlife photographer may not be able to move close enough to his subject to take a satisfactory photograph with a standard lens, so his kit will always contain one or more telephotos. (Left) using a standard lens in a room like this, you would only get the far wall into the picture. A wide-angle 'sees' most of the room.

The principal reasons for changing lenses

As noted previously, the standard 50mm lens casts an image with a magnification factor of ×1 as seen in the viewfinder—i.e. objects are viewed
at the same size as they appear to the naked eye. Some photographers
maintain that the covering power of the 50mm lens closely resembles the
effective angle of human vision, claiming that although the eyes have in
fact a much broader sweep than the 46° of the 50mm lens, they concentrate
on a relatively narrow portion of it. Others argue that the eyes are rarely
at rest, and believe that the angle of view of a 35mm lens (62°) is more
like human vision in the real world, as opposed to the ophthalmic
optician's clinic. One of the great advantages of the interchangeable lens
system is that every individual can choose his own 'standard' lens. It is
certainly sound practice to settle for a lens of moderate focal length to be
kept on the camera for general photography, changing to a longer or
shorter lens whenever necessary—whether for a single exposure or for a
day's shooting—and then reverting to the chosen standard lens.

Wide-angle lenses

A wide-angle lens will be preferred to any other when the photographer is
working in a restricted space, but needs the covering power he would
normally get from a standard lens.

Telephoto lenses

The photographer mounts a telephoto lens on his camera for the same
reason that people use opera glasses—its primary purpose is to magnify
distant objects when they cannot be more closely approached for a better
look.

Other reasons for changing lenses

Experienced photographers can usually estimate with reasonable accuracy
the focal length of the lens used to take a given picture. This is because
lenses have highly individual characteristics which become more and more
pronounced as extremes of focal length are approached. Sometimes these
properties can be emphasized for their own sake, although this requires
restraint on the part of the photographer if visual sensationalism is to be
avoided.

Focal length and depth of field

The shorter the focal length of a lens, the greater the depth of field in the
images it produces. Lens aperture and focusing distance still exert some
influence, but with lenses of around 28mm focal length or less, for
average subjects and lighting conditions, the effects of focal length will
be the dominant factor and will tend to swamp the other considerations.
With a fish-eye lens it is hardly necessary to focus at all, so great is its
depth of field: this is known as the 'pan focus' effect.

Conversely, depth of field diminishes progressively as focal length
increases, so that with telephoto lenses it may be very restricted. If objects
in the image area are at very different distances from the camera it will
often prove impossible to get them all in focus. There is no technique
that will eradicate this problem without changing to a lens of shorter
focal length, but there are two partial solutions. The first is to minimize
the problem as far as possible by using fast film and slow shutter speeds
(the camera may have to be mounted on a tripod), making it possible to

Other factors being equal, the field of sharpness increases as focal length gets shorter. A 35mm lens was used here and the picture is sharp from foreground to horizon.

reduce aperture to its minimum, then use the depth of field scale to make the most economical use of the available depth of field—possibly by focusing on the hyperfocal distance as described on page 63. The second solution which only works for subjects not requiring focus in depth, is to make a virtue of necessity by exaggerating the shallowness of field: a telephoto lens used at close range and maximum aperture restricts depth of field so far that everything behind and in front of the point focused on makes a pleasant soft contrast with the razor-sharp outlines of the subject itself. Accurate focusing is of the utmost importance when this technique, which is known as differential focusing, is employed. A telephoto lens may sometimes be chosen for no other reason than that the photographer wishes to exploit this quality.

Focal length, perspective and camera-to-subject distance

Neither the camera nor the human eye has any means of altering perspective without shifting position: substituting one lens for another of different focal length cannot alter the relative size of objects as seen from a given vantage point (the shift lens is an exception). The difference between lenses lies in what they include in the image area and what they omit. A wide-angle lens includes more of a scene at the edges of the frame than a standard or longer lens. The effect of this on the image depends on what these additional corridors of view contain: if they simply extend the existing scene vertically and horizontally in a more or less flat plane the difference may not be very striking at first sight, although in capable hands it can bring about a subtle change of emphasis. But if new foreground material is included the whole balance and composition of the image can be dramatically altered, and a sense of perspective may be introduced that was previously lacking (which is not the same as altering perspective).

The combination of immense depth of field with a wide angle of view gives wide-angle lenses a capacity for highlighting perspectives which the eye normally ignores: when an object comes very close, the human eye tends either to look straight past it at something else, or to concentrate on it and disregard the background, which will be confused on account of our binocular vision as well as out of focus. A photograph presenting a one-eyed view of both object and background in sharp focus obliges us to compare them. The result is one of the most familiar and easily recognized

Focal length and perspective: the two pictures on the left were taken with a 20mm lens from close up, those on the right with a 200mm lens standing back. Observe how a flat surface changes hardly at all, while a subject which has depth is dramatically different.

characteristics of wide-angle vision: a humorous or grotesque effect, particularly unflattering as a technique in portraiture.

The potential subject matter of any photograph taken from a given point is what you see around you, in whole or in part. Telephoto lenses have the power to isolate small parts of the scene and turn them into full-sized images. In theory it should be easy to see any vista as a patchwork of telephoto images, but in practice this is difficult, partly because a good lens has a higher resolving power than the eye and can turn a distant smudge into the detailed likeness of an object, and partly because the mind's eye cannot easily pull forward and magnify a small rectangle so that it obliterates vast tracts of foreground. And unless the foreground can be eliminated, the telephoto effect is not achieved.

Telephoto lenses are, as mentioned earlier, primarily telescopes adapted for photographic use; but in bringing the subject closer to the observer they bring the background closer as well. One effect of perspective is that the difference in the relative sizes of two objects widely separated in front of the lens is much less when both are a long way from the vantage point. These relative sizes are retained in the telephoto image, and this, to the unpractised eye, makes the objects seem much closer together than they actually are.

A photograph taken with a telephoto lens of any focal length is identical to a cropped enlargement made from another photograph taken from the same position with a lens of shorter focal length. Depth of field may be different, however, and the cropped image becomes progressively degraded by evident grain as the degree of enlargement increases.

It has been assumed so far that the photographer has a choice of lenses in his kit but is imprisoned in a cell with one window. Photographers often are restricted in this way—the holidaymaker recording the view from his hotel window, the aircraft enthusiast confined to the public observation platform, or the architectural photographer commissioned to photograph in a small room—but there are also situations in which he can move about freely, and this greatly increases the creative potential of interchangeable lenses: because perspective alters with every step you take.

This means that the relative proportions of any two or more objects can be varied, and of course any one of them can be kept at a constant size in the viewfinder if the photographer wishes. When a single individual or thing is the subject of a photograph one perspective may be considered more pleasing than another. The classic example of this is the formal portrait: it is generally agreed that with a moderate telephoto lens, i.e. one of about 70-100mm focal length, used at a reasonable distance so that the subject fills the frame, the most natural and flattering perspective is achieved. Sometimes lenses in this range are even referred to as 'portrait lenses'.

More complex subjects comprising several distinct elements can be variously interpreted. The actual size of objects becomes less and less restricting the greater the range of focal lengths available to the photographer: one object can be made either to dominate the scene or to recede into insignificance; a small person can be made to tower over other much taller people; fine old buildings can be made to huddle in the backyard of brash new high-rise blocks, and so on.

SMC Pentax lenses

Standard lenses

	Angle of view	Forward projection when focused on ∞	Filter size
SMC Pentax-M 40mm f/2.8	56°	18mm	49mm
SMC Pentax 50mm f/1.2	46°	48.5mm	52mm
SMC Pentax-M 50mm f/1.4	46°	37mm	49mm
SMC Pentax-M 50mm f/1.7	46°	31mm	49mm
SMC Pentax-M 50mm f/2	46°	31mm	49mm

Anyone new to 35mm photography is advised to start with one of these lenses and use it for a good three months or so before investigating lenses of other focal lengths. The standard lenses represent the single most versatile group, and their relative simplicity of design and construction makes them economical when compared with other lenses of similar speeds.

The 40mm f/2.8 'pancake' lens is especially recommended where compactness is important, and its slightly wider angle of view makes it a good choice for the sort of subject that is likely to be encountered when travelling—buildings, impressive vistas and groups of people—while remaining adequate for portraits.

The four 50mm lenses differ in their maximum aperture, and hence in both bulk and price. For a first-time buy, unless you are quite certain that you will be taking a lot of pictures indoors or in poor light, the f/2 or f/1.7 lenses are recommended, as they are both small yet fast enough for use in most situations without flash or tripods.

A standard lens can cover most situations, particularly if you can choose how far you are from the subject.

Wide-angle lenses

	Angle of view	Forward projection when focused on ∞	Filter size
SMC Pentax-M 28mm f/2	75°	41.5mm	49mm
SMC Pentax-M 28mm f/2.8	75°	31mm	49mm
SMC Pentax 30mm f/2.8	72°	39.5mm	52mm
SMC Pentax-M 35mm f/1.4	62°	64.5mm	58mm
SMC Pentax-M 35mm f/2	62°	42mm	49mm
SMC Pentax-M 35mm f/2.8	62°	35.5mm	49mm

Some photographers prefer to treat lenses in this range as standard, but it is a matter of personal preference.

Wide-angle lenses are not difficult to handle, offering good depth of field but without taking in so much subject matter that composition becomes a problem (c.f. the cautionary note on ultra-wide-angles).

If you have previously been used to photographing with a 35mm compact camera you might prefer to buy a 35-40mm lens for your SLR rather than one of 50mm focal length, as the lens fitted to such cameras is almost invariably in this region. Otherwise these make a good choice for a second lens to be added when you are thoroughly familiar with your first.

Subjects and situations that generally respond favourably to wide-angle coverage include landscape, architecture, anywhere among crowds such as on the streets or at carnivals etc., most forms of travel photography, group portraits and portraits of individuals in which the sitter is one element among many, and any situation in which space is restricted or subject matter widely dispersed.

'M' series lenses are very light and compact for their focal length, which makes them particularly suitable for photographers who go out and about in pursuit of original images.

Landscape taken with a 35mm lens.

Ultra-wide-angle lenses

	Angle of view	Forward projection when focused on ∞	Filter size
SMC Pentax 15mm f/3.5	111°	81.5mm	Built-in
SMC Pentax 18mm f/3.5	100°	61.5mm	Built-in
SMC Pentax-M 20mm f/4	94°	29.5mm	49mm
SMC Pentax 24mm f/2.8	84°	41.5mm	52mm

Lenses in this category can be difficult to use—not in terms of physical handling, but in terms of image structure and composition. Their wide angle of view brings an enormous area of subject into the viewfinder and images with deep front to back interest can be hard to integrate. Without actually looking through the viewfinder it is not easy to visualize the effect of such wide viewing angles. However, they can be used to create an impression of immeasurable spaciousness in landscape photography or to encompass the extremities of great buildings from quite close by them, and when handled with assurance by an experienced photographer it may not be evident to the uninitiated that any special lens has been used at all. Alternatively, the 'distortions' inherent in much ultra-wide-angle photography can be created easily by less experienced photographers.

The purchase of a lens in this category should therefore be approached with a good deal of thought. Photographers who have found by experience that they tend to favour wide-angle viewing will enjoy the challenge of putting one of them to work. Price inevitably increases as the extremes of focal length are approached (more so at the telephoto end), so these are definitely for the enthusiast. However, the 24mm f/2.8 is reasonably priced and may be used with one of the Pentax dedicated flash units fitted with its wide-angle adaptor—the widest-angle lens which can be used with direct flash.

A striking ultra-wide-angle view of London.

Moderate telephoto lenses

	Angle of view	Forward projection when focused on ∞	Filter size
SMC Pentax-M 85mm f/2	29°	46mm	49mm
SMC Pentax-M 100mm f/2.8	24.5°	55.7mm	49mm
SMC Pentax-M 120mm f/2.8	21°	63mm	49mm
SMC Pentax 135mm f/2.5	18°	85.9mm	58mm
SMC Pentax-M 135mm f/3.5	18°	65.7mm	49mm

As an alternative to the wide-angle lenses listed on page 131 these lenses, which are intermediate between standard and genuine telephoto, represent an ideal choice of second lens for the photographer who has fully explored the performance limits of his first acquisition. They will be preferred by photographers who, on looking through their stock of pictures, find that they instinctively want to crop superfluous material or vacant areas at the edges of the frame. In particular, this is the portrait range—ideal for both the posed portrait and for the candid but bold character study taken at close range among throngs of people. In either case the differential focusing capability is a significant advance on that achieved with standard lenses, and perspective of full-frame subjects is more natural.

The 120 and 135mm lenses have enough magnification to be valuable in sports and theatre photography and can be very effectively used to isolate details in architectural work. The usefulness of all of these lenses is further extended by the use of Pentax electronic flash units having a telephoto adaptor.

Moderate telephoto lenses can be used for general photography by those who favour them, but are especially valued for portrait work, whether fairly formal or candid.

Telephoto lenses

	Angle of view	Forward projection when focused on ∞	Filter size
SMC Pentax-M 150mm f/3.5	17°	75mm	49mm
SMC Pentax 200mm f/2.5	12°	145mm	77mm
SMC Pentax-M 200mm f/4	12°	111mm	52mm
SMC Pentax 300mm f/4	8.5°	188mm	77mm
SMC Pentax-M* (M-star) 300mm f/4	8.5°	132mm	77mm

These versatile lenses are designed principally with the sports and nature photographer and photojournalist in mind—in other words, the photographer who needs a compromise between compactness and light weight, with enough speed for action photography by available light and genuine telephoto reach. They are also particularly favoured by photographers with a flair for graphic design, who exploit the telephoto foreshortening effect to bring a degree of abstraction into certain types of image—this is more manageable with the lenses listed here than with the longer ones.

The lenses in this category are suitable for hand-held shooting at moderate shutter speeds, but a tripod should be used for speeds slower than 1/125 sec with a 150-200mm lens and 1/250 sec with a 300mm lens (this is because in telephoto pictures the effects of camera shake are magnified in the same ratio as the subject).

Rear Converter K T6-2×

When fitted between lens and camera body this telephoto converter doubles the focal length of any lens with which it is used. Designed for optimum quality with lenses of 135-300mm focal length, it extends the use of such lenses into the ultra-telephoto range and thus saves both money and weight. It can also be used with zoom lenses, and is obviously a good investment for anyone who has only occasional need of ultra-telephoto reach or who undertakes lengthy field trips on foot. Because of the increase in the focal length of the combination, f/numbers marked on the aperture ring of the main lens are 2 stops too wide; e.g. the maximum aperture of an f/4 lens is f/8 when used with the Rear Converter.

One use of a telephoto lens is to experiment with the design aspect of picture composition.

Ultra-telephoto lenses

	Angle of view	Forward projection when focused on ∞	Filter size
SMC Pentax-M 400mm f/5.6	6°	276.5mm	77mm
SMC Pentax 500mm f/4.5	5°	440mm	52mm
SMC Pentax 1000mm f/8	2.5°	738mm	52mm

Lenses in the ultra-telephoto range are for professional and dedicated amateur sports and wildlife photographers, and for photojournalists covering events which for one reason or another cannot be approached closely. Although the 400mm lens especially is lightweight and can be used for hand-held shooting, these lenses can be hard work to use—not, as in the case of the ultra-wide-angles, for compositional reasons but because at great working distances the slightest camera movement is magnified, and fast shutter speeds cannot often be selected as the maximum aperture of very long lenses is relatively small. Also, the greater the subject distance the more obtrusive can slight atmospheric dust and haze become.

These drawbacks are the necessary price to pay (along with the financial one) for the performance offered by lenses in the ultra-telephoto class: the 400, 500 and 1000mm lenses magnify distant objects 8, 10 and 20 times respectively.

To facilitate handling, the 500 and 1000mm lenses are equipped with a built-on sight, and the 1000mm also features rack and pinion focusing and a special tripod as an optional extra.

Very long telephoto lenses can isolate details or patterns from a considerable distance: a 400mm lens has made this more than just a conventional picture of boats.

Reflex telephoto lenses

	Angle of view	Forward projection when focused on ∞	Filter size
SMC Pentax Reflex 1000mm f/11	2.5°	248mm	Built-in/ 52mm
SMC Pentax Reflex 2000mm f/13.5	1.3°	530mm	Built-in/ 52mm

These extremely powerful lenses, known as 'catadioptric' because they employ both reflecting (catoptric) and refracting (dioptric) elements, offer exceptionally high-quality telescopic performance combined with relative compactness. A 1000mm lens magnifies distant objects 20 times, which is enough to focus objects invisible to the unaided eye; the 2000mm lens doubles this again. The 1000mm f/11 reflex is only 248mm long, while its conventional dioptric competitor is very nearly three times as long, although it has the advantage of extra speed.

As the design of reflex lenses does not allow for an adjustable iris diaphragm, four neutral density filters are built into each of these lenses for exposure control. The arrangement of mirrors and glass elements interrupts the light path in such a way that out-of-focus highlights take the form of rings rather than discs—an unavoidable tell-tale effect, but not by any means an unpleasant one. The light path twice doubles back on itself, enabling the 2000mm (over 6½ft) focal length to be contained within a unit that measures 180 × 530mm (about 7 × 21 inches).

Needless to say these lenses, though masterpieces of applied optical technology, are very expensive and not likely to be useful in amateur photography except in the case of the very dedicated wildlife or sporting photographer.

Eclipse of the sun photographed through a 2000mm lens: the subject comes up good and big in the frame.

Zoom lenses

A zoom lens is one in which focal length can be varied continuously within the stated limits. The optical quality of early zoom lenses was undeniably poorer than that of 'prime' lenses—i.e. those of fixed focal length—but nowadays the problems of extending optimum performance over a reasonably wide range of focal lengths have been largely overcome. Any remaining quality differential between zoom and prime lenses is so slight that it is only likely to be noticeable in certain forms of scientific photography; for commercial uses zoom lenses are good enough. Furthermore modern zooms are much lighter and more compact than their antecedents.

Their great advantage, of course, is that a single lens can be carried instead of a number of prime lenses, and that intermediate focal lengths can be selected. In any situation demanding fast responses this flexibility is invaluable, as it enables the photographer to follow his subject along the optical axis as well as laterally. Used with a camera offering automatic exposure, such as the ME Super, a zoom lens permits a degree of control that would have been inconceivable a few years ago.

Early zoom lenses were mostly in the medium telephoto range, but the

This special effect can be achieved by zooming during the exposure—very impressive when well done. Normally you use the zoom facility to frame the subject before exposure.

use of computers to do much of the spadework involved in lens design has led to the development of high-quality wide-angle zoom optics, and there are now no gaps in the Pentax range between 24mm ultra-wide-angle and 600mm ultra-telephoto. One of the lenses that spans the standard range, especially the 40-80mm, is a perfectly realistic first-time buy for the ambitious photographer who wants something more than a standard 50mm lens.

Altering the focal length of a zoom lens is by one of two systems: in the 'one-touch' system a single collar is used to control both zooming and focusing (push/pull to zoom out/in, rotate to focus), whereas in the independent two-ring system each of these functions is separate. The two-ring system used in the wide-angle zooms is more compact, and instant readiness to refocus is less crucial on account of the greater depth of field offered by short focal lengths. The one-touch system is employed in lenses that extend into the telephoto range, where simultaneous framing and focusing is more likely to be required. Of the two Pentax zooms that extend right across the standard focal lengths, one (the 35-70mm) uses the one-touch system and the other (40-80mm) uses the independent two-ring system.

If you have decided in principle that you wish to acquire a zoom lens, the final choice should be based on the same considerations as would guide your choice among prime lenses. Once a focal length has been chosen for a given shot, the lens behaves in all other respects like a fixed lens of that focal length.

	Angle of view	Forward projection when focused on ∞	Filter size
SMC Pentax-M Zoom 24-35mm f/3.5	82.5-64.5°	48mm	58mm
SMC Pentax-M Zoom 24-50mm f/4	84-46°	71mm	58mm
SMC Pentax-M Zoom 28mm f/3.5-50mm f/4.5	75-46°	52mm	52mm
SMC Pentax-M Zoom 35mm f/2.8-70mm f/3.5	62-34.5°	76mm	67mm
SMC Pentax AF Zoom 35-70mm f/2.8	63-34.5°	76.5mm	58mm
SMC Pentax-M Zoom 40mm f/2.8-80mm f/4	57.2-30.9°	76mm	49mm
SMC Pentax Zoom 45-125mm f/4	50.5-20°	127mm	67mm
SMC Pentax-M Zoom 75-150mm f/4	32.1-16.5°	111mm	49mm
SMC Pentax-M Zoom 80-200mm f/4.5	30-12°	141.5mm	52mm
SMC Pentax Zoom 135-600mm f/6.7	18-4°	582mm	52mm
SMC Pentax Reflex Zoom 400-600mm f/12	6.2-4.1°	108mm	67mm

Special purpose lenses — Macro and Bellows

	Angle of view	Forward projection when focused on ∞	Filter size
SMC Pentax-M Macro 50mm f/4	46°	42.5mm	49mm
SMC Pentax-M Macro 100mm f/4	24.5°	77.5mm	49mm
SMC Pentax Bellows 100mm f/4	24.5°	40mm	52mm

The macro lenses have much in common with regular lenses of the same focal length; the difference is that they can focus on far shorter distances and are designed to offer optimum performance in close-up photography. They are not, however, restricted exclusively to close-up use: having the capacity to focus on any distance up to infinity they are very versatile and can be used for portraits, landscapes, architectural work and all forms of general photography within the limitations imposed by the relatively small maximum aperture of f/4.

It is in the realm of nature that macro lenses really come into their own. The 50mm f/4 can be used in conjunction with the 49mm Reverse Adaptor to magnify objects to greater than life size on the emulsion, making images which, when enlarged or projected, reveal with extraordinary clarity details which are normally below the threshold of human perception. The 100mm lens, with its 24.5° angle of view, effectively makes close-ups of subjects that cannot be brought right up to the lens, which makes it easier to focus on animals in their habitat without disturbing them, and to take genuine macrophotographs of subjects separated from the photographer by physical barriers such as the bars of a cage.

The 100mm f/4 Bellows lens is designed to give greater than life-size images of tiny objects when used in conjunction with Auto Bellows M, or almost life-size images with Bellows Unit K (see page 142).

For more about the techniques of close-up and macro photography see pages 217-219.

A beautiful abstract composition made by photographing the frost pattern on a window with a macro lens.

Special purpose lenses—Fish-eye and Shift

	Angle of view	Forward projection when focused on ∞	Filter size
SMC Pentax Fish-eye 17mm f/4	180°	34mm	Built-in
SMC Pentax Shift 28mm f/3.5	75°	92.5mm	Built-in

The fish-eye lens has an angle of view of 180°; that is, the edges of the frame contain subject matter that is actually in the focal plane: everything in between, perceived by the eye as the inside of a cosmic hemispherical bowl, is flattened into a two-dimensional image. If you stand opposite a long row of buildings and sweep your eyes from one end of them to the other, you can obtain some impression of how and why the fish-eye lens apparently curves straight lines.

The effect is dramatic or even surreal, and the lens requires very careful handling or the elements of the picture can lack co-ordination. However, the fish-eye lens is a powerful and essentially photographic creative tool.

The SMC Pentax Shift lens is in some ways the exact opposite of the fish-eye: instead of exaggerating perspectives it 'corrects' them, presenting an image which matches what we *think* we see, but not what we actually *do* see. With a focal length of 28mm its angle of view is 75°, which is a good working length for most architectural photography.

The remarkable feature of this lens is its ability to shift the optical axis so that it is no longer perpendicular to the film plane, which has the effect of tilting the subject plane about its optical centre. The lens barrel can be rotated to adjust the direction of tilt, so that horizontal as well as vertical converging lines can be rendered parallel. The use of this lens in architectural photography is described in detail on page 207.

The characteristic fish-eye effect: the human eye cannot take all this in without moving.

Close-up accessories

Close-up lenses

SMC close-up lenses, which can be attached to the front of any lens of compatible size in the same way as a filter, offer a simple means of increasing the closest focusing distance of a lens. The TTL metering system of the ME Super takes care of the exposure problems that arise when working close up: the open-aperture metering capability of the main lens is unaffected.

Magnification—the ratio of the size of an image at the focal plane to the actual size of the object—is irrelevant in normal photography but very important in macro and close-up work. It gives a clearer indication than focusing distance of what a lens or a combination of lenses and other accessories can do.

$1\times$ (or 1:1) magnification gives an image at the film plane that is exactly life size: in the context of 35mm photography the image area will be exactly filled by an object that measures 24×36mm. To photograph objects smaller than this, if the frame is to be filled, magnification must be increased—$2\times$, $3\times$, $4\times$ etc. Objects larger than 24×36mm need to be reduced, and the degree of reduction is expressed as a fraction of $1\times$ — $1/2\times$, $1/4\times$, $1/7.5\times$ and so on.

The power of supplementary lenses is measured in dioptres. The following table gives some examples of the effect of combining the Pentax range of supplementary lenses with the more common prime lenses.

Type	Strength (dioptres)	SMC Pentax lens	Magnification
S25	3	20mm f/4 50mm f/1.2, 1.4, 1.7, 2 40mm f/2.8 35mm f/2, f/2.8	$1/7\times$ $1/2.7\times$ $1/2.7\times$ $1/2\times$
S40	2	35mm f/2, f/2.8 40mm f/2.8 50mm f/1.2, 1.4, 1.7, 2 85mm f/2	$1/3.2\times$ $1/3.5\times$ $1/3.5\times$ $1/1.7\times$
T80	1	85mm f/2 135mm f/3.5	$1/4.2\times$ $1/2.6\times$
T95	0.9	135mm f/2.5 200mm f/4	$1/3.7\times$ $1/2.6\times$
T160	0.6	100mm f/2.8 100mm f/4 Macro 135mm f/3.5	$1/3.5\times$ $1/1.7\times$ $1/4.9\times$
T183	0.5	135mm f/2.5 200mm f/4	$1/5.5\times$ $1/3.8\times$

Extension tubes and bellows units

Focusing a lens consists of altering the lens to focal plane distance (see page 16). When working at close range the amount of forward movement required is much greater than at normal subject distances. To build the capacity for such large movements into the lenses themselves would make them impossibly cumbersome; however the extra distance can easily be introduced between lens and focal plane by the use of extension tubes or bellows.

The tube sets offer extensions in a series of fixed steps, although by using them in various combinations together with the focusing movement of the lens you can obtain almost continuous focusing. Bellows units perform the same function, with the advantage that their extension is continuously variable and the disadvantage that they are more expensive to buy.

Listed below are current Pentax extension tube sets and bellows units; in those designated 'auto' there is a diaphragm coupler to permit open aperture metering, while stop-down metering is necessary with manual accessories.

Auto Extension Tube K50 (50mm)
Auto Extension Tube K100 (100mm)
Auto Extension Tube Set K (12, 19 & 26mm: total 57mm)
Manual Extension Tube Set K (9.5, 19 & 28.5mm: total 57mm)
Helicoid Extension Tube K
Auto Bellows M (38-176mm)
Bellows Unit III (32-137mm)

Reverse Adaptor

When magnifications of greater than 1× are required all lenses provide better results if mounted in reverse, whether or not they are used in conjunction with extension tubes or bellows. The Reverse Adaptor K is available in 49mm and 52mm sizes, and screws into the filter thread at the front of the lens, enabling the lenses to be bayonet-mounted back-to-front. No diaphragm coupler is incorporated and stop-down metering must be used. When mounted in reverse with neither tubes nor bellows any lens can focus considerably closer than when mounted normally.

Macro Focus Rail

At very close focusing distances depth of field is so restricted that accurate focusing is critical and can be upset by the slightest movement of the camera in relation to the subject. The Macro Focus Rail enables the position of lens or extension tube to be precisely set in relation to the subject and film plane, so that the problem of magnification being altered by refocusing of the lens is overcome. It can be tripod-mounted, and will be found indispensable when a specific magnification is required or whenever magnification exceeds 5× or so.

Slide copiers

Slide Copier M (for use with Auto Bellows M)
Slide Holder 1×, K (for use with Auto Extension Tube K or Extension Tube K)
Slide Holder K (for use with Macro 50mm lens and Auto Extension Tube no. 3)

For duplication of valuable slides, which is a sensible precaution if they are to be sent out, e.g. to publishers, friends, or simply for reversal printing.

Slide Copier M and Slide Holder K permit a degree of magnification, so that the composition of slides can be improved by cropping if required.

Macrophoto Stand/Lighting Table

For ultra-close-up and macro work. The Macrophoto Stand offers continuously variable magnifications from $1/2\times$ to $1.9\times$ (with Fine Focus Adjustor III, 50mm f/4 Macro lens, Auto Extension Tube Set K and Reverse Adaptor K), or from $0.7\times$ to $3.1\times$ (when used with Auto Bellows M). A reversible grey/black stage plate is included, of which the grey side is of 18% reflectivity, making it suitable for substitution exposure readings as described on page 69. The Lighting Table is equipped with a transparent glass stage plate enabling close-up subjects to be illuminated from below by a built-in tungsten lamp. For brighter lighting at exposure time there is a built-in mirror which can be used to reflect light from other sources, including electronic flash. 35mm and 6×7 slide carriers are available as optional extras for slide duplication.

Copy Stand III & IIIP

Ideal for copy work (see page 216 for copying techniques). Model III is fixed, while Model IIIP is portable, the base doubling as a carrying case. Both have a reflector of 18% reflectivity for substitution exposure readings (see page 69). A table clamp is available for fixing Copy Stand III to a table with top less than 6cm thick.

Microscope Adaptor K
Microscope Lens Adaptor K

Enable Pentax SLRs to be used with microscopes or special purpose objective lenses, for photomicrography.

A snowflake, magnified by a factor of 5 on the negative: the camera reveals the beauty of microscopic structures.

Focusing attachments
SMC Correction Lenses
Correction Lens Adaptors
For spectacle wearers, correction lenses in 8 dioptres are available, ranging from −5 to +3 dioptres.
Magnifier
An eyepiece attachment which magnifies the central part of the focusing screen for critical focusing.
Refconverters (right-angle finders)
Especially useful in macro work at low or otherwise difficult angles. The simple Refconverter is for use with cameras having no viewfinder display, as the image appears reversed. With Refconverter II and Refconverter-M the image is correctly oriented so that exposure information can be easily read.
Eyecups
Facilitate viewing and prevent stray light entering the camera through the viewfinder and so upsetting the metering system.

Sundry accessories
Stereo Adaptor
Stereo Viewer II
For making and viewing 3-dimensional slides. Available in 49mm and 52mm sizes for attachment to the filter thread.
Mount Adaptor K
Enables screw-mount Takumar lenses to be used with bayonet-mount Pentax camera bodies; not equipped with a diaphragm coupler.
6 × 7 Lens Mount Adaptor K
Enables 6 × 7 lenses to be used with bayonet-mount Pentax 35mm camera bodies; not equipped with a diaphragm coupler.

Protective accessories
Cases
Standard and soft cases are available in many different sizes for camera bodies fitted with various lenses, and for lenses on their own. There is also a range of hard cases for those who need to carry all their equipment on assignments or leisure travel.
Lens Caps, Lens Mount Cap K and Body Cap K
Spare protective caps as supplied with all new equipment.
49mm-52mm and 52mm-49mm Adaptors
Permit filters of either size to be used with lenses having filter thread of the other size.

Hand-held Exposure meters
Spotmeter V/Spotmeter V-FL
Digital Spotmeter
Designed for the professional photographer, these exposure meters offer fast and accurate response within a very narrow angle of acceptance, making it possible to meter subjects which are too far away for TTL metering, or where unusually complicated lighting prevails.

Landscape

1. Monument Valley in the warm red light of a clear evening

2. A slow shutter speed has recorded movement in the leaves

3. Industrial landscape can be especially dramatic: underexposing by a stop or so increases the impression of airlessness and pollution

4. Monotony can give strength to the landscape

5. Bizarre lighting effects in the Antarctic

6. A characteristic wide-angle lens shot

7. Low raking light gives modelling to the land: undulating landscapes are best photographed soon after sunrise or before sunset

8–9. Two telephoto lens shots, showing its capacity for apparently altering the relative sizes of objects (top) and for compressing the subject against its background (bottom)

10. An old bomb crater, seen through a wide-angle lens

11. The form and texture of the willows in winter are the subject of this almost monochromatic composition

1. Monument Valley

2. West Indies

3. Steelworks, Pittsburgh, Pennsylvania

4. Southern England

5. Antarctica

6. Lake Dal, Kashmir

7. Maiden Castle, Dorset (Iron-age fort)

8. Western Australia

9. Scotland

10. Southern England, near Portsmouth

11. France

Architecture

1. Standing back from the subject has enabled the photographer to keep the camera level, avoiding the distortion caused by converging verticals

2. A shift lens has been used here to keep the columns parallel, while the fluting is beautifully picked out by the angle of the sunlight

3. The tiled floor provides a sufficiently interesting foreground to allow the camera to be held level

4. As it was impossible to avoid converging verticals, the photographer has chosen a camera angle that will exaggerate them for effect

5. Large areas of glass can give a translucent, weightless impression

6. Graphic, almost abstract compositions may be appropriate to modern architecture: a high contrast ratio makes this easier.

7. During an exposure of approximately 20 seconds a colour shift occurred due to reciprocity failure, which accounts for the blue coloration of the floodlights.

8. The Pompidou Centre is a favourite subject for photographers and responds well to informal treatment

1. Palmyra: Great Colonnade and Triumphal Arch, 2–3 century AD

2. Baalbeck: Interior of the Temple of Bacchus, 2nd century AD

3. St Paul's Cathedral, London—South aisle

4. York Minster – pier with stained glass reflections

5. Franklin National Bank Buildings, New York

6. The Guggenheim Museum, New York—interior and skylight

7. Battersea Power Station, London

8. Pompidou Centre, Paris

Nature

1. Colour is a very important part of the living world—the fly agaric looks dangerous, and it is

2. The monarch butterfly, taken with a macro lens

3. Green lacewing fly, lit by electronic flash

4–5. Complementary impressions of nature, the poppies vibrant and colourful, the sunflowers withered and dying

6. Slight underexposure emphasizes the shafts of sunlight in dark woodland

7. A wide-angle lens was chosen to make the subject stand out boldly against its habitat

8. Lioness on a termite mound, watching for prey: an obvious case for a telephoto lens

9. Hippopotamus group with Nile cabbage, seen through a telephoto lens

10. Birds silhouetted against the setting sun—a stunningly atmospheric telephoto lens shot

1. Fly agaric, *Amanita muscaria*

2. Monarch butterfly, *Danaus plexippus*

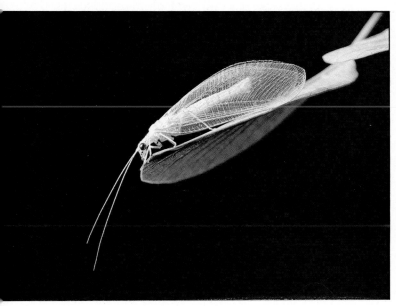

3. Green lacewing fly, *Chrysopa* species

4. Sunflowers

5. Poppies

6. Woodland

7. Horned poppy, *Glaucium flavum*

8. Botswana

9. Nile

10. Patna, India

Still life

1. A collection of bottles, photographed on daylight-type transparency film using a powerful electronic flash unit with diffuser, placed to the left of the camera

2. Still lifes are usually arranged in the studio, but need not always be— interesting compositions may crop up anywhere

3. A very carefully arranged studio shot—note how carefully the glass has been lit to make it stand out against the dark background, which itself would be ideal for a title or advertising copy

4. Another first-class studio shot, originally conceived as a jacket photograph for a book about pasta cookery

5. The main light is placed behind and to the right of the subject, giving it a clear outline; a small frontal fill-in light picks out surface detail

6. *L'oiseau de feu* lamp with its own illumination; the main photographic light is above and behind the lamp

1. Bottles

2. Shop window

3. Home-made wine

4. Pasta

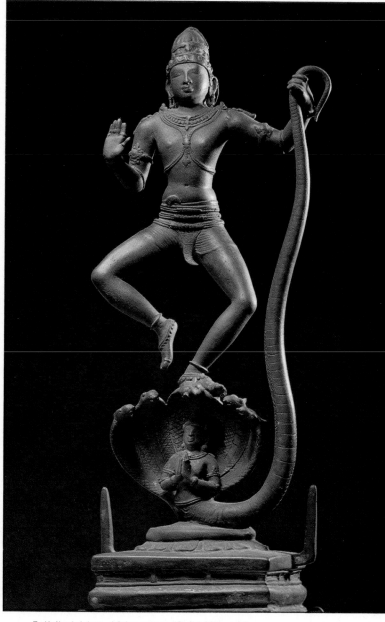

5. Kaliyakrishna, 10th century (Delhi Museum)

6. *L'oiseau de feu* lamp by René Lalique

Technical portfolio

1. The starburst filter is often over-used, but adds a wonderful glitter to this impressionistic nature photograph

2. Take city lights at dusk to preserve some light in the sky

3. The greenish tinge of the street lights is caused by reciprocity failure during the long exposure necessary to catch a lightning strike

4. Wide-angle lenses often draw clouds out into a striking fan shape

5. A strange powdery/smoky effect, caused by some of the snowflakes being way out of focus, characterizes this chilly railway scene

6. Underexpose by one or two stops when photographing flames—but better still, bracket your shots if you are ever lucky (?) enough to get into a situation like this

7. An unusually effective rising pan

8. Powerful electronic flash has swamped the artificial light sources in the picture, so that daylight-type transparency film could be used

1. Starburst filter

2. Johannesburg at dusk

3. Reciprocity failure and lightning; Durban

4. Wide-angle lens; Western Australia

5. Chur, Switzerland

6. Bunbury, Western Australia

7. Munich

8. Electronic flash; Yorkshire

12 Advanced Photography

Approaches to photographing people

The hunter

There are many approaches to photography, any one of which will, under the right conditions, produce good photographs. There is the purist approach of a Cartier-Bresson, who perhaps without the knowledge—and usually without the co-operation—of his subject, using the simplest and most inconspicuous equipment, stalks like a hunter the perfect instant—the perfect combination of action, composition and light which fixes for ever the elusive moment in an evocative image of compelling human significance.

The director

At the far end of the spectrum is the controlled approach of the advertising photographer, who works within a brief which has been agreed by all the other parties to create the finished advertisement. The creative art directors and copy writers at the agency, who have refined an idea and proposed it to the account executive, who in turn has convinced the client that *this* is the best possible way to persuade the public: they all depend on the creative and technical skills that enable the photographer to produce under rigorously controlled conditions a final product which will—hopefully—seem as real and convincing to the viewer as the 'moment of truth' of a Cartier-Bresson image.

Most photographers, whether advanced amateurs or professionals, will find that their work is not usually at either extreme, but combines some of the possibilities and requirements of each approach. The hunter's instinct can be sharpened by experience, and his speed of response to any situation is now accelerated by the instant readiness of a modern automatic camera like the Pentax ME Super.

The purpose of this chapter is to explore some of the techniques which can be used to obtain improved photographic results through the control afforded by the ME Super and the diversity of 35mm materials. These are techniques which have been developed by professionals, who must always produce the right picture at the right time (or almost always—every professional has heard the fateful word 'reshoot' at one time or another).

Portraits

There are a lot of ways of photographing people, in different situations and for different purposes: street activities, special occasions like weddings, sporting events, and so on. Making portraits was one of the first and is still among the most important uses of photography. The ability of the camera to study the human face and record its nuances of emotion and expression in detail, added to the convenience of being able to make as many prints as are needed, has given portrait photography enormous potential. It has one particular advantage: that a reasonably good likeness of the sitter is more or less guaranteed—which not all painters can boast. But to develop that immediate advantage towards the creation of a deeper and more meaningful image of the subject is the real challenge. A good portrait can be much more revealing of the real person than just a good likeness.

Posing the subject

First, as a portrait is being made with the active approval and help of your subject, the photographer's role is principally that of director: the hunter element is limited to being alert for the fleeting expression that escapes and reveals the sitter's real personality—preferably the best side of it. The lighting and composition are under your control, and the sitter will be glad of suggestions as to attitudes and posture: tell him or her whether to lean forward or back, where to redirect his glance for each new exposure, and so on.

If, as is likely, your subject is not an experienced model used to obeying the photographer's orders, do not overwhelm him with instructions because he will only become stiff and self-conscious. A moderate telephoto lens is very useful in portraiture, giving you a large image from further away. This has two advantages: first, the image is not distorted in the way a face appears to be if you move in close with a normal or wide-angle lens; and second, you are working at a comfortable distance from your subject, and many sitters find this less disconcerting. A tripod may be useful with the telephoto lens, to minimize camera movement (unless you have either enough light to use short exposures, or else are using only electronic flash, which will freeze any movement). It has another advantage: you may be able to look directly at the sitter instead of through the finder, and this leaves you free to talk with him or her while watching for the best attitude or expression.

It is often an advantage to work in surroundings that are familiar to the sitter as these can contribute to both mood and personality. A farmer, after

A portrait may show the sitter without props (right) so that pose, lighting and expression are the key ingredients. If props are used (left) the picture may tell more of a story.

all, will feel and look right out of doors in his working environment. A business man at his desk, a pianist at his piano—these portraits are more than a face, they are part of a life. Of course one must take care that odd objects do not become distracting—they should all form part of the overall composition. If a purely formal portrait is required, a plain area of wall or a non-patterned curtain, or even a roll of wrapping paper can be pressed into service as neutral background.

Lighting

The lighting for portraiture needs to be simple and manageable, as well as showing your subject to his best advantage.

The light from a window makes a useful point of departure when thinking about portrait lighting, because it is readily available and we are so familiar with it that it usually looks natural. One classic version of this is to arrange the sitter so that the window is above him and slightly to the side—this arrangement has been used for centuries by artists. They call it 3/4 lighting. It shows the cheekbone structure, darkens the eye-sockets, and gives modelling to the mouth and chin, as well as shadowing the side of the nose.

Changing the position of the sitter and of the camera in relation to the window can give a surprisingly broad range of lighting effects, even though the window itself is fixed. If the subject moves even a couple of paces away from the window while the camera moves towards it, the light becomes soft and flattering. It is especially useful for a girl, as although it shows the bone structure less strongly, skin texture is smoothed out and improved. The background tends to become dark, because it is so much further from the window, so you may want to supplement the light on it, or bring a bright background into a position close behind the sitter. On the other hand, if the subject moves close to the window while the camera is moved into the room, the effect can vary from a delicate edge-lighting— often delightful in profile—to a complete silhouette if the exposure is held down, or a high-key back-lit effect if the exposure is increased by two to four stops.

The center-weighted metering system of the ME Super will take care of most situations, but with an extremely back-lit subject, it is essential to go in close and see what the reading is from the face alone. Use the manual exposure mode to retain the correct exposure if the reading from the shooting position differs by more than the two stops that are within the exposure compensation range of the camera. Another professional tip: girls' faces seem to look cleaner and prettier if they are slightly overexposed, i.e. by $\frac{1}{2}$ to 1 stop.

The effects of window light can be varied further by the use of reflectors— a sheet or a newspaper can be useful—and you can judge the effect by half-closing the eyes if you are standing back from the camera rather than looking through the viewfinder.

If, instead of having to rely on a window, you have an artificial light source which is also large and flat but has the advantage of being mobile, the technique of portrait lighting can be further developed. One simple and portable accessory is a special umbrella, white on one side and with silver fabric on the other, which can be mounted on a stand at any height and angle. A light mounted on the handle illuminates the inside of the umbrella, which then becomes a light source with qualities equivalent to the window, but fully adjustable. For example, it can easily be positioned to give the classic 3/4 light described earlier; but if it is swung round so as to come more from the side, the face will seem much harder and bonier, and the skin rougher. This can be appropriate for a man, but is not (traditionally, at least) what is wanted for a girl's face. For a girl, swing it into a position almost in line with the camera, but just slightly above it. The face will magically smooth out, with highlights appearing in the eyes, and the cheekbones showing just a hint of modelling as the light falls away at the sides. This may be enhanced by a bit of shadow make-up along the jaws and about the eyes—a trick known to professional models. Look at some advertisements for beauty products and see how many of them have been lit this way; sometimes you can even see the reflection of the umbrella in the model's eyes.

The use of two umbrellas, one on either side of the camera, will soften the light even more. But two lights used this way must be *very* close to the lens, or they will throw conflicting shadows. The general rule is that no matter how many lights are actually used, they should have the effect of one main light plus natural reflections of it. Crossed nose shadows will ruin the most attractive subject.

Another thing to beware of is throwing light up into your subject's face: this give a horror effect that may be appropriate for Dracula but not for the average sitter. The human race has been looking at light coming from the sun and the sky for so long that it only looks natural coming from that direction. There is a classic photograph set up with hard lighting from below, and reproduced as a negative. The viewer accepts it as a positive light from above: an interesting exploitation of the capacity of the human brain to re-interpret what it sees.

However, *soft* light from below can profitably be used to fill in shadows: a useful technique is to have girls sit with their elbows on a table covered with white paper. That degree of reflection seems only right and natural.

Once the main light is properly placed, other lights—if they are available—may be added. A basic kit for amateurs interested in serious portrait photography might consist of perhaps five or six soft-spot mushroom lamps in clamp-on holders, together with some folding stands and an umbrella. One or two spots are aimed into the umbrella to make a primary source, plus one or two on the background if necessary to help with separation or simply to add interest. One can be bounced off a card near the lens to fill in shadows, and one placed high up and slightly behind the subject adds life to the hair, and, depending on which way he is looking, may either give a helpful highlight on the cheekbone (although it must almost always be kept off the nose), or, if he turns away, can give a line of light along the whole profile.

Opposite page: lighting for portraits. Photo *a* was lit by a main light from the right with fill-in from the left; *b* is similar but with the background also lit; *c* shows the hard effect of a single light at right-angles; *d* is like *b* but with stronger fill-in lighting, and in *e* and *f* note the subtle difference caused by a change of camera angle.

a

b

c

d

e

f

One of the advantages of this kind of arrangement is that the subject is free to move and turn in the course of several shots, without the lighting having to be rearranged all the time—it is a time-consuming and distracting business, both to the photographer and his subject.

There is, however, a rhythm which often happens in portraiture, in which a series of shots may seem to come to a natural end. When this happens, and the subject begins to get bored or even to freeze, sometimes a break to change the lighting is helpful. You may then be able to come back to shooting with renewed vigour and enthusiasm on both sides.

Light sources discussed so far may be either daylight or tungsten, and of course for colour film these should not be mixed (see page 10). Occasionally when shooting daylight film near a window you may find that some tungsten lighting inside the room will give an unobtrusive orange glow, but usually the effect is only distracting. Certainly if you are working with tungsten film any daylight should be avoided. Close the curtains or window blinds completely, otherwise you may get some unexpected blue highlights in eyes or hair. Your own eyes will not see it— they have a wonderful capacity for adjustment to changes in the colour of light—but it is astonishingly evident on the film.

Electronic flash, on the other hand, being the same colour as daylight, may well be used with it. Out of doors, especially in harsh daylight, a flash unit on the camera can fill in and soften shadows (see page 120). Also, when working near a window, it can be helpful to use a flash unit mounted on the camera but with the head tilted up to give a bounced light off the ceiling. Sometimes you may even prefer to work under the umbrella with the flash directed at that—but you do not want the fill-in light to be too strong. Experimenting with these effects is essential, because with flash your eye cannot see what the combination of light is producing for the camera.

The psychology of portraiture

Once your lighting is arranged, the way the subject feels is the next most important thing. Here a little psychology can be most useful. Few people are ever totally happy about their appearance, and any aspect of this that needs to be fixed—hair disarranged, say, or a change in eye make-up— needs to be underplayed and treated as just a minor change that will help the overall effect. Anyone watching a fashion photographer working with a model, whose ego may be as fragile as anybody else's, will hear a steady litany that goes something like: '. . . that's wonderful . . . turn a little bit, that's marvellous . . . tilt your head a bit, fantastic . . .' etc. That steady flow of reassurance and flattery is exaggerated, of course, like everything in fashion, but the principle applies to working with any subject. A man being photographed also needs some running commentary—presumably in different terms—to reassure him that he is doing what is best for the camera, and to prepare him for each shot: people do not like to feel that they are being caught off-guard.

General advice on portraiture

Some of the minor tricks of the trade may not be immediately obvious. For example, have the subject of a formal portrait sit with his shoulders turned to one side or the other. It will make him seem much more natural as he then turns his head and eyes towards the camera. The height of the camera can be of crucial importance—it rarely works well higher than the subject's eyes, as it not only masks the eyes themselves but also makes the nose look longer. Particularly for a man, the camera position can be fairly low: the viewer of the finished picture then has to look up at him and he seems to gain height and authority. Another useful trick—and one which is drilled into politicians appearing on television—is to lean forward a little, towards the camera: this helps to establish contact with the viewer, and can have the added advantage of minimizing any paunch. There is another tiny relaxing movement which will help to soften an expression that has become a bit fixed, and that is moistening the lips. This not only adds a touch of highlight, it also relaxes the muscles around the mouth.

Diffused light from the front gives life to the contours of the body, while black cards on either side darken the outlines. The whole picture has been slightly underexposed.

Informal outdoor portraiture

Photographing people out of doors can be a means of making an entirely different type of portrait. It immediately becomes more natural and casual, and it is easy for the subject to relax. Obviously it is best to avoid harsh sunlight—especially in the middle of the day, direct sun is unlikely to be very flattering. But later in the day the sun may provide a very interesting light, falling direct on a rugged masculine visage or used as back-lighting for a girl's hair. Certainly there is no need nowadays to stick to the old rule of having sunlight over the photographer's shoulder: study instead the effect of having the light come in from several angles. One device is to move your subject into the shade, perhaps of a wall or tree. Use the ME Super to take a reading from the face only; the fully lit background will become high-key by comparison, and can be less distracting and more decorative. Your eyes may tell you that your subject is too dark, but exposure compensation makes up for that on the film.

If the general arrangement is attractive but the light on the face is not quite right, a reflector catching the sun can be used to give a different effect. One made of aluminium foil will be brilliant and directional, whereas a white card is softer, so you can choose the effect you like best if you have both. (Crumple the foil thoroughly before you glue it to a backing.) Again, if the reflector becomes the main source of light on the face its position will be critical. The same principles apply as with artificial light: it must come from above or to the side, not from underneath—tempting though it may be to rest the reflector on the ground, taping it to your tripod will probably be a better alternative. If the reflector is only softening and filling in the shadows, its position is not so critical.

Natural reflectors, such as white walls or the sand on beaches, are often a great help. Their abundance in the Mediterranean region is one of the features that make it such an agreeable place to photograph: the whole

Informal outdoor portraits—the technique shown below is simple but makes a lot of difference: turn your subject away from the sun, which casts terrible hard shadows, and instead illuminate the face with a plain white card reflector.

quality of the light there is different, with so much of it being reflected. In less favoured climates this feeling of all-round light can be simulated artificially. A good way to do this is to use flash-on-camera as a general fill-in, being careful not to let it become strong enough to be noticeable. Stop down by one or two stops, otherwise the effect may be overpowering. The flash unit will need to be set in one of its manual modes.

Children

Taking pictures of children is probably the single most popular application of photography. Every detail of a child's life can be fascinating, and the sentimental value of a pictorial record grows with the years as a child develops and changes. But the ability to catch the right expression, to show the true personality of the child, will depend on the development of a technique of working with children so that they think they are doing what *they* want to do—not what fond parents or the photographer are trying to make them do.

That is why a rewarding time to photograph children is when they are busy with their own affairs: building a sand-castle, concentrating on a board game or upside-down in a jungle gym. This is where the art of the hunter-photographer comes in: the photographer needs to be an inconspicuous presence which can almost be forgotten while the really important game continues. Sometimes, obviously, a suggestion or a word of praise helps but generally speaking, if they are happy and busy, the less

Informal pictures of children are easier to get than formal ones, but that does not excuse laziness in other aspects of picture composition, such as filling the frame and choosing a background that does not distract.

 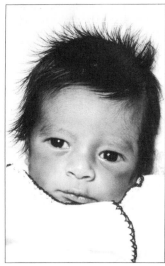

This rather surreal scene looks like something out of *Peter Pan*, but the boy was only playing with his father's shirt. Children at play present many fleeting images.

Bounced flash used as the main light source for a new-born baby. The flash unit was on its manual setting. An automatic flash would have produced a greyer result.

obtrusive the photographer is, the better. Some children have been ordered about so much while being photographed that they begin to hate it and this shows in their expression. The automatic exposure function of the Pentax ME Super is invaluable for this kind of shooting as the photographer is free to concentrate on timing and composition and can forget about exposure and reciprocity. One especially useful piece of equipment is a zoom lens, e.g. the SMC Pentax-M 35mm f/2.8–70mm f/3.5 one-touch zoom.

This will save a lot of conspicuous moving around and needless time wasting: you will be able to reframe the image instantly from, say a half-length portrait to a close-up when the child's expression momentarily makes the most interesting subject matter for a picture—or vice-versa when 'body language' is transmitting a clearer message. Children move quickly, so speed of response is a vital factor: a zoom lens perfectly complements the automatic exposure facility in such unpredictable situations. The main thing in these situations is to be ready for whatever happens—and this includes a readiness to wait for things to develop. One of the great virtues of the hunter must be patience. This certainly applies to anyone photographing children.

This is the case to an even greater extent when you are asked to photograph children who are strangers, whom you know only slightly or not at all. An extra degree of patience is required in getting to know the child well enough, and in developing his confidence in you sufficiently so that he can relax and be himself. Sometimes it helps to show interest in his possessions; sometimes children show curiosity about your equipment, and that can be satisfied by asking them to help with a lens cap, or looking through the finders themselves—a wasted frame or two of yourself staring into the lens can be a quick way to show them that this is a mutual enterprise, in which they are an equal partner.

It is sometimes even more difficult to gain the co-operation of a parent than of a child—it is all too common for eager parents to try to get their child to smile when he may not feel like it because they want him to be immortalized as a happy, smiling child; they may even resort to issuing edicts '. . . just you do what he tells you to do . . .' etc., which will rouse self-respecting individuals of any age to sulky rebellion. Time spent in explaining tactfully to parents exactly what is going on, pointing out that it is much easier for the child to concentrate if only one adult is talking to him, and that their role is ideally one of passive reassurance and a quiet presence in the background, can ease the situation enormously.

One distinguished photographer who specializes in children has gone so far as to arrange his studio so that as soon as some degree of confidence has been reached he and the child are left alone together for the actual photography, while the concerned parent can watch the proceedings from another room, through an unobtrusive window.

One important factor in getting good pictures of children is your point of view. You wouldn't expect the best picture of adults to be taken from ceiling height; similarly, it pays to get down to the child's height, whether by kneeling, sitting or lying on the floor. It not only provides a more human, normal view of the child, but psychologically it is likely to be good for the child—some photographers benefit from it too—to see you rolling about on the floor. Sometimes the situation can be formalized to a certain extent by having the child sitting in a chair, a high chair if he is the right age; this is also a useful device to cut down his range of movement if you want, say, a range of close-up expressions.

Babies

The above remarks apply mainly to older children. When photographing babies the situation is in some ways much simpler, because they are not only less mobile but less conscious of photographers and their cameras. Here the participation of the mother is absolutely essential, because she is the baby's universe and his whole being reacts to her. A full record of a baby's early life can make one of the most rewarding of photographic projects. The means can be of the simplest—there is no need for complicated lighting and posing. The natural window light described for portraits (page 179) is a suitable starting point, and can give an almost Vermeer-like quality to a mother and child near it. Added to this a small flash bounced off the ceiling, or even occasionally direct, or held a foot or two away from the camera on a flexible lead when the action justifies it, as in the bath, will cover one group of activities. Then using a fast tungsten film for the evening rituals, with a minimum of bright lights and commotion to disturb a baby going off to sleep, you can often get the pictures you want at the same time as keeping both mother and baby happy.

Advertising photography

Beauty and fashion photography for publication is one of the most highly specialized forms of photography. If it is for advertising, it will follow very closely the concepts already agreed by the agency and the client, quite probably expressed in detailed drawings, or 'layouts', which will include every detail and measurement that is required for the finished work. These layouts must be followed exactly, as they have taken into account the space available in the magazine, the number of words in the copy, the positioning and size of the headline, and the proportions and positioning of the various agreed elements of the picture.

Many editorial photographers also function very efficiently in the advertising field. They may well have been called in for discussions at the very beginning to help set the direction of a campaign, to add their own creative ideas before the details have been fixed and agreed by all the other parties. In any case they are willing to accept the limitations imposed by a layout, in order to gain the efficiency which comes from using an approach which has been agreed in advance to be the best one possible. After all, if he is asked simply for a picture of a beautiful girl, it is very difficult to know what is really envisaged. But if he is asked for a photo cropping to a horizontal 10in wide and 7in deep close-up of a blonde, chic mother-type with shoulder-length hair and with a 3-4 year old boy in a red shirt slightly out-of-focus in a playground situation—then he can deliver what is needed to accompany the headline and text. All he has to do is deliver a marvellous photograph within that brief: the hunter element is reduced to a minimum, the control element is nearly 100%.

The professional approach

In putting together a photograph like the one outlined above, the professional photographer starts with model selection, which is perhaps the single most important factor in a beauty or fashion shot. Everybody may be in on the decision, but the photographer's preference, with any luck, will be the deciding factor. He probably knows the possible choices better than anyone else, how they look and how they work.

If the advertisement is to appear in the spring it will have to be shot in the winter, so it may be necessary to plan on a studio shot, with a props assistant finding and hiring whatever playground equipment is most suitable—perhaps a slide, as then the boy will naturally be up near the model's head. Blue background paper, (it comes in rolls 9 or 12 feet wide) perhaps sprayed to give a vaguely cloudy, more natural effect must be hung; and then there are the test shots to try out the best imitation sunlight effect, to get the best texture and highlights on the hair, to check the degree of loss of focus on the boy at various distances from the mother, to make sure there are no shadows falling on the 'sky', and so on. The lighting will be electronic flash, which has eliminated many of the old difficulties of subject movement, change of light colour with voltage fluctuations and so on, but which does require testing to make sure that the effect of the flash is the same as the modelling lamps, as well as to check the exposure.

Once all is ready in the studio, the preparation of the model may involve both a make-up expert and a hairdresser. The make-up is sometimes a source of friction, as any successful model will have arrived at a make-up style which she finds best for her face. The make-up expert may have

An example of an advertising photograph set up by a team of professionals.

different ideas, and it can be a diplomatic problem for the photographer to negotiate a suitable solution.

The hairdresser, by his very profession, is likely to be a good psychologist himself, besides having technical abilities. He will also be keenly aware of the brief time during which hair will retain its best conditions and shape. So the general arrangement should be checked by bringing in the model before her hair is quite finished, in order to perfect the lighting, try out fans or the flapping cards which may be needed at the last moment to bring life into the hair, and take some Polaroids to be sure everything is still functioning perfectly. Then the final make-up touches and the last brush-out, probably in front of the camera, and suddenly the models are alone with the photographer and his lens.

The organisation of a professional sitting has been described here not only because some of the details may be helpful, but to emphasize the amount of planning and thinking ahead that is involved. That is an important lesson to learn: that thinking ahead, planning, testing and checking out are never wasted in studio photography, and may be critical to the success of a photograph.

Fashion

Fashion photography, whether editorial or advertising, tends to be freer in its execution, because advertising pages will appear alongside the editorial ones and must compete in terms of vitality and creativity. There are certain requirements common to both—the clothes must look good, the girls must look good, and the backgrounds should add to the general atmosphere of luxury and elegance.

A fashion model is invariably tall and slim, always over 5ft 8in, occasionally 6ft and over, with a small head set on a long neck. The clothes often have to be pinned in to fit them (as the house models who show the garments to buyers have a more normal build) and this may be done with any combination of clothes pegs, bulldog clips, Scotch tape and string—because the clothes only need to look right from one angle: that of the camera.

The girls will have worked out their best make-up and hair styling, and as soon as they arrive at the studio will start to perfect them. They may arrive with their hair already in rollers, or they may use heated rollers in the dressing room. Their make-up will be designed to improve their looks for the camera, not for the street, so their cheeks may be darkened to emphasize the cheekbones and minimize the jaws, the nose may be darkened along the sides with a highlight down the middle to narrow it, the eyes will be shadowed and lengthened with eye-liner, and a better shape of mouth may be outlined, filled in and highlighted with lip-gloss. The overall effect to the eye may be startling, but to the camera the best points are exaggerated, the worst ones hidden.

A good fashion model is a joy to work with. She will enter into the spirit of the clothes, and repeat and refine any movement that is showing them to advantage. The rapid whirl which makes a skirt stand out, standing on tip toe to make the legs look longer, and the bringing of all the elements—eyes, body, expression—together, timed for the click of the camera: these become second nature to the experienced fashion model. Her skills complement those of the photographer in a joint creative act. It is no accident that so many models marry photographers: they make good teams.

The nude

The nude has been a favourite subject for artists for many centuries, and of photographers for at least a hundred years. But photographing a nude really well is even more difficult than drawing or painting one, because the realism and detail of a photograph not only exaggerate defects in the model's body (and no model is without them), but make it difficult to achieve the slightly abstract beauty which is the difference between a truly artistic nude and an ordinary naked body.

Choosing a model

In choosing a model, obviously one looks for a softly curved body, with breasts which are not too heavy. Dancers often make good models, having good control over their muscles, and leading disciplined lives which keep them visibly fit. One model, who did both nude and fashion modelling, once said that nudes were by far the harder work, as every bit of the body had to be just right, every muscle under control for the photograph. Clothes were easy to show off, by comparison.

In advertising photography, models and props must often look unnaturally perfect.

The gesture of raising the arms gives a flattering outline to heavy breasts.

In fashion work the photographer must have total control over everything—difficult enough with a single model, but to control three of them is quite an achievement.

Posing

Any movement which lengthens and tightens the muscles is likely to look attractive in nude photography, pulling in the belly muscles, clenching hip muscles, and extending feet to lengthen the leg lines. One natural movement, which shows off beautiful breasts and can also lift heavy ones to a lovely line, is to raise the arms back over the head.

It is important to keep a casual atmosphere—once the model is reassured that this is not an erotic encounter, and that you just want her to look beautiful for the camera, she is more likely to relax. An atmosphere of tension, and a lot of fussing about with lights and posing can upset even an experienced model. No one is quite as confident without their clothes on, and you need to protect that fragile ego. Physically the studio needs to be really warm—warmer than you would choose for yourself—if the model is to relax and be comfortable. After all, the last thing you want is goose-pimples.

It is important to ask the model to come in really loose clothes and underclothes. The marks from elastic look awful, and will last a long time. Do not let your model make the same mistake as the one who was sent back to the dressing room to rest and get rid of such marks—and then sat on a cane-bottomed chair!

Working out of doors, if you can find a warm, secluded place without observers, can provide a splendid way of photographing nudes. Sun, sand, rocks and whitewashed walls can show off a girl's body beautifully. If you are on holiday it is worth waiting a few days until she is naturally brown. Make-up can help, but it is a laborious job to try to do it all with cosmetics.

A suitable location may not be easy to find, but if you stumble upon one it will often be better to make a note of it and go back another day— this time properly prepared and with the model suitably dressed as mentioned above.

Lighting

The most interesting light for nudes is likely to be early or late in the day, but always—even when you are not actually photographing—be on the lookout for the backgrounds and the lighting effects which will be favourable later for shooting: reflections in mirrors or water, or light through trees or Venetian blinds. These can be turned to advantage whenever you spot them occurring naturally, but can be very difficult to set up in a studio, no matter what the facilities.

Always when photographing nudes, either in the studio or out of doors, it is useful to study the effect of warm filters on your subject. The Kodak Series 81 to 81 DE are designed to change artificial light (such as photo-floods) which is slightly too blue for tungsten films to the right colour and they are different shades of warm brown. Used over the lens in any light they give to the eye an overall brown tinge, and this is often effective in smoothing the skin and helping it to look golden and sunny. Experiment, though, to see which effect you like best. They require a slight increase in exposure, but this is taken care of by the TTL metering system of the ME Super. If your finished transparencies still look cold, you can try projecting them through the same warm filter, or duplicating them using a light source that is warmer in tone.

Candid Photography

Photographing people as they go about their business in streets, markets and other public places provides some of the most interesting material that one can bring back from a holiday, but is equally fruitful much nearer home. The personalities to be observed in a London street market like Portobello Road, or in one of the huge wholesale markets, offer splendid subjects for 'candid' photography.

Of course, tact and discretion are always useful both at home and abroad: no one likes to feel like an animal in a zoo, pinned by an intrusive camera. But a variety of approaches can help. One is the use of a long lens, so as to study people's faces from a distance. Another is to be quick about the actual photography: planning your shot, then making any camera preparations while looking the other way. Then you need only raise the camera at the last moment, leaving much less time for self-consciousness or resentment to occur. Here of course the ME Super is in its element.

The opposite reaction is also encountered: some people just love to be photographed, and will co-operate with a smile at the slightest suggestion. Your own smile, with its implicit recognition that people like to be friendly if given the chance, can be your best introduction in any language.

Photographs for publication

The legal status of the photographer, in the West at least, is roughly that anything that happens in public is fair game to be photographed and published for pictorial or editorial use. But be careful: if a picture is to be sold for advertising, posters or other *commercial* use, you will be asked by

A medium telephoto lens is useful in candid photography to concentrate on interesting detail.

For street scenes, a standard or wide-angle lens is the best lens to keep fitted to the camera.

the purchaser for the signed consent of anyone recognizable in the photograph, and without that permission the photograph will not be saleable. Models who are being paid to pose are used to signing a release form giving you all rights to their photographs, and these forms are sometimes quite elaborate. But occasional subjects may be quite happy to sign a brief handwritten note saying that you are free to use the photographs you have taken of them on that date for any purpose, and legally that is usually sufficient.

If you do sell a photograph for either editorial or commercial use, consider carefully just what rights you are selling for the agreed fee. A 'one-time non-exclusive world rights' sale preserves your right to sell the photograph elsewhere. If you sell, 'all rights' as some companies ask, the payment should be proportionately higher.

Anyone used to our freedoms in Western Europe must realize that elsewhere in the world, photography is not accepted quite so casually. Subjects like soldiers, airfields, bridges and shipping may turn out to be off limits in various countries, and a question or two about local rules may save you from having your film confiscated, or even some equipment impounded.

Photographing the stage

Theatre photographs are a special field. Taking pictures during a performance is normally prohibited, to avoid annoyance both to the actors and the audience. Therefore it is best to arrange to work during rehearsals if possible. But rehearsals are tense times for the actors and director too, and if you do get permission to attend, it is best to sit in the stalls with a telephoto lens, on a tripod if possible or else braced on the seat in front of you, as the work-lights are likely to be less powerful than the eventual stage lighting. You will need to be prepared for long dull stretches when nothing seems to happen—with occasional fascinating picture possibilities.

Near opening time, there may be a photo-call. With the costumes, decor and lighting added, this is the best time to work. Then it is in everybody's interest to get the best pictures possible, and they are ready to co-operate, moving about as needed. Even close-ups on the stage are now feasible.

Amateur and fringe productions can be fun to photograph, and they may well cheerfully go along with your requirements, especially if they can have some of the results for publicity or personal use. Here the lighting may be quite basic, and some judicious adding of key lights or softening reflectors for close-ups may be advisable.

It is worth remembering that practically all publicity requires black and white prints, preferably 8 × 10 glossies. Any colour you do will be primarily for yourself, unless they have money available for front-of-the-house colour prints. Magazines use colour, but they work so far ahead that it is nearly unheard of to sell an unplanned theatre story to a magazine.

Pop music performances, with their spectacular lighting effects, can make good photographic material, and there are seldom any restrictions on the use of cameras. But to record successfully the colour and drama of these productions you need to be fairly close to the action. Although a telephoto lens can get you a larger image, it is generally a stop or two slower than a normal lens, which may bring you into the region of under-

Exposure can be difficult to judge with spot lighting, but this type of shot is most impressive when it succeeds.

exposure. Even center-weighted exposure metering cannot read the correct exposure for a small brilliant area surrounded by black (but see page 69); so it may be worth your while to give as much exposure as you can (taking into account camera movement, etc.) on fast Ektachrome and then get your laboratory to test the results of pushing a few frames at the beginning of the roll by a couple of stops. You will then be able to judge whether the rest of the roll should be forced the same amount, or less, or whether it is hopeless. There will be more contrast than usual, and the further the film is forced the more the colour may vary, but in a really difficult situation it is better to have a less-than-perfect image than no image at all. One word of warning—this technique requires that all the film be exposed in the same manner. Otherwise you may ruin good shots trying to save tricky ones.

Sports

Sports photography has been revolutionized by the 35mm SLR camera—it is the ideal tool to cover the fast, often distant and unpredictable action of sporting events, whether swimming, football, motor racing or any other. The wide range of available lenses, combined with fast shutter speeds and the automatic Winder ME-II let one get closer to the centre of action than ever before.

It is always valuable to attend practise sessions, when there is less tension in the air and fewer people around. The chance to get good pictures of the sportsmen increases; a skater or gymnast, for example, may be glad to have some photographs of himself, and glad to co-operate in making them as good as possible.

But some photographs derive their interest from the tension and atmosphere of the big occasion—boxing and wrestling for example. In these the sense of occasion is important—and showing the referee or part of the crowd in the shot helps to create this.

Above: sports photographers are obviously interested in the personalities, not just the action. Here, a telephoto lens has caught the concentration in Princess Anne's face. Opposite page, top: a fast shutter speed is often effective in water sports photography, freezing every droplet of water and catching the pattern of light in the breaking waves. Bottom: in other sports events it may be strength rather than movement that the photographer seeks to convey.

Here again we have the option of going for the available light, with the sense of atmosphere and reality it gives, or flash on the camera with its sharp, action-stopping detail—invaluable for boxing shots, for example, when it can even catch blood and sweat flying under the impact of a hard punch. In this sort of action timing must be reduced to a matter of reflexes: your finger must be pressing as the blow starts, or it will all be over before you shoot. It helps if you keep shooting with both eyes open, to judge your timing better—remember, if you *see* something dramatic in the finder, you do not have it on the film.

The wide-ranging games like football and hockey are perhaps the most difficult. The SMC Pentax 400-600mm Reflex Zoom f/12 is ideal for sports photography, being exceptionally compact for its focal length and light enough for hand-held shooting. Newspaper sports photographers produce those marvellous close-ups with very long lenses, using a motor-drive to give as many shots as possible of any promising action. Very often they have their film pushed to squeeze out 2 to 4 extra stops of speed—and then there is a brutal selection process which discards hundreds of pictures for each one used.

Shots of track and field events are simpler: you know where and when the critical moment will be and can prepare for it. Prefocusing on a hurdle or a finishing tape is a simple technique: then you can concentrate on getting that moment of ultimate effort. It is often effective *not* to use your highest shutter speed, as a little blur heightens the effect of movement. And, of course, when runners, racing cars etc. are moving past you follow them in the finder and shoot while panning—the background will streak and give an impression of speed while the subject stays sharp. It is not only the absolute speed of the subject that determines sharpness, it is how far the image moves on the film while the shutter is open, and panning with the movement reduces this. The technique applies even more to auto racing, where a stationary camera only records a blur of colour—which may sometimes be attractive, but not for too many shots.

Russian gymnasts photographed by the stadium floodlighting. Here you want a zoom lens or a ringside seat, or both.

Weddings

Weddings are another occasion which deserve all the planning and all the skill you can bring to them. If you are doing the whole 'official' record, it is a great responsibility; if anything goes wrong with the photographs, the pictorial record of the single most important day of the bride and groom's life is lost forever. So do not even offer to do it for nothing unless you are really confident of your ability to cover the whole story quickly, thoroughly and well.

But if there is a professional to take over that responsibility, it can leave you free to do a lot of the informal, friendly shots that he is likely to miss. For one thing, he may for safety's sake depend a good deal on his on-camera flash, which means that most of his pictures will have clear but uniform lighting. If you can work with available light, you can add an extra dimension of reality because your pictures will reflect the real situation—even with fragments of movement, backgrounds out of focus and so on. Get as much information ahead of time as possible, finding out just how the reception will be organised—indoors, or on a terrace or under a marquee—because this will determine your choice of film, though it is likely to be the fastest available, whether for daylight or artificial light.

Every incidental situation that you can get will be worthwhile: the bride getting ready, arriving at the church, the group photo arranged by the official photographer but shot from the side before they are ready, and again after they think it is all over. When the confetti is being thrown open up the aperture, as a slow shutter speed can show an attractive blur. Close-ups of the bride's hand and the bouquet are essential—here again a zoom lens is a help, just as it is for pictures of the couple leaving.

The key to all this is *anticipation*—thinking ahead to what is going to happen next, so that you will be in the right place, with the right lens to cover it; thinking already of the next event and planning to be ready for that. It does not leave much time for champagne—but this can slow up a photographer's reflexes anyway.

Always try to get good simple photographs of the main participants in a wedding ceremony.

Slide duplicating

It is possible and may be highly desirable to duplicate transparencies—perhaps because you have one perfect original you would like to protect, or because you have an original that might be improved with cropping, or even because you want to create a totally new photograph by combining two or more originals. Successful duping requires a well-controlled technique, but this is worth perfecting for yourself if you want to do a large number.

For just an occasional dupe it is probably easier to go to a commercial laboratory, but this gets very expensive in any quantity.

Pentax make various slide-copiers (see page 142), for use with a bellows unit or extension tubes—for optical reasons, you will have an image the same size as the original when the film plane to subject distance is four times the focal length of the lens. Electronic duplicating machines are manufactured for professionals who must make a lot of dupes.

The question is, how best to reproduce the original image. The first difficulty is that if you use ordinary film, it will increase the contrast of the original. Depending on the subject, that may not matter much, or may even improve it. But accurately to reproduce originals, Kodak make a duplicating film with lower contrast (see page 220) but this is only sold in 100ft lengths, which must then be loaded into cassettes to be used in the camera. One can approximate the effect by shooting Ektachrome one stop over-exposed, with the processing time *cut* correspondingly. Whatever material you try, it must be tested and used methodically, so that every step can be reproduced or altered as required, and careful notes kept so that it can be set up in precisely the same way days or weeks later. You will want to note down every bit of information you can for later reference, so that you do not have to start again from the beginning.

Once you have a standard procedure that gives you satisfactory dupes, you can use the process for improving your photos. One situation in which this arises concerns the rescue of underexposed transparencies. You may have shots which are too dark to show properly on the projection screen, but which do contain detail in the shadows which can only be seen when the slide is held up to a bright light. Giving dark originals a stop or two more than normal exposure when duplicating them can often save shots which are otherwise lost—you can tell in advance by looking with a strong light to see if the image is really there: if it is not there, of course, nothing will help.

Multiple exposures are made simple by the duping procedure. For example, to superimpose a face on a landscape, just wind the shutter with the rewind button depressed (to disengage the sprockets) and set up the second image as you want it. Fireworks are a natural for this technique, and you can add different coloured filters behind each original, to make them even more spectacular. You may want to change the size or cropping of one or more of your originals, too: it can be done, but needs care:—it is very distressing to discover that an edge of a picture, intended to be solid black, has actually printed through and shows the edge of the mask. Bracketing of exposures, variations in filtration and composition—every experiment is worthwhile, as long as you keep a record so that you can repeat the best results.

Photographing things and places

Professional photographers usually enjoy their work. There is tremendous satisfaction in firing the shutter on what you know is going to be a good photograph. Of course firing the shutter is the easiest part of taking a picture, and some people even make a mess of that. Knowing that the photograph is going to be worth the film it is taken on comes from experience and practice, because, like all art forms, photography involves a process of constant learning.

The debate over whether or not photography qualifies as an art has been going on since the first photographs were taken, and no doubt will continue as long as there are cameras. But there is an important difference between photography and the other visual arts. A painter can use his imagination and skill to create any image he wants, but the photographer is restricted to what is in front of his lens. At the lowest level this makes photography easier than painting, because the camera performs mechanically what the painter needs considerable skill to achieve. In this way, the main limitation of photography is also its greatest asset. But this limitation imposes on the photographer the need to select something to point his camera at.

This need to select is at the basis of every aspect of photography; every photograph involves a series of selections of subject matter, viewpoint, equipment, material, composition, lighting and exposure. Where the amateur will simply point his camera and shoot, the professional will unconsciously or consciously make a series of selections or decisions. Before firing the shutter he has already covered all the angles, so that he knows exactly how he wants the photograph to turn out. Most professionals are framing up shots in their mind's eye all day long—they are always looking for photographs, even if their nearest camera is miles away.

Viewpoint

An essential part of his interpretation consists of the viewpoint the photographer chooses. One of the common faults of the amateur is to

There is mild humour in the viewpoint relating the main elements of this shot.

An unusual abstract view of a pylon, lit by direct electronic flash.

release the shutter without pausing to ask, 'am I in the best position for this shot? Should I be five yards to the right, and so avoid some obstacle in the foreground? Should I be nearer the subject?' The viewpoint controls the perspective of the shot, but it also contributes a great deal to the composition. One of the commonest faults is the failure to look right into the corners of the frame as it appears in the viewfinder. The Pentax ME Super has a clear bright viewfinder, but, like other SLR cameras, has to be held right up to the eye; and it takes a surprising amount of eyeball-swivelling to look carefully into all four corners of the frame. Another factor to consider when choosing the viewpoint is how much of the scene in front of him does the photographer want to include—in other words, what focal length of lens should he select? The viewpoint and the length of lens depend on each other to produce the framing and perspective of the shot.

Materials

Having selected a subject, a viewpoint and an appropriate lens, the next question is, what sort of film to use? For a professional, the choice of colour or black and white is usually made by the client; for the amateur it is a matter of taste and expense. Until recently, those who like to do their own developing and printing usually preferred to work in black and white, as most colour processes were too complicated for home use. Over the past few years the introduction of simpler chemical processes and the relatively inexpensive colour print drum processors have made colour printing at home a practical proposition. The choice between colour negative and colour transparency material (slides) raises various problems. Colour negative film is slightly cheaper, and making a print from negative film is quite a lot cheaper than making one from a transparency. On the other hand, colour negatives are more or less meaningless unless printed, and are unsuitable for reproduction in a magazine or book. But they have the advantage, like black and white negatives, of offering some control at the printing stage: minor errors of exposure and colour balance can be corrected. With a colour transparency everything has to be right before the shutter is pressed; once it has been processed, it is too late to improve it (except by the fairly elaborate means described on page 200).

Lighting

Lighting is the very essence of photography—a photograph without light is a contradiction in terms. Light is generally considered in terms of its direction and its quality. In outdoor work, the direction of light is usually dictated by the position of the sun, which takes us back to the selection of the appropriate viewpoint. In some cases it means waiting until the sun has moved into a favourable position. In the studio there is more flexibility, as the lights can be moved around at will. Even outdoors, many photographs need a certain amount of manipulation of the available light, using reflectors such as tin foil or white card, or even fill-in flash.

The direction of light reveals the form of the subject. A light behind the camera will show detail and shape, but without much feeling of depth. A light behind the subject will reduce it to a silhouette, while a light from the side will reveal contours and allow shapes to appear three-dimensional.

One of the ways to appreciate the effects of different lighting is to look at a scene in terms of its shadows. Just as shading is one of the first things to learn in drawing, so photographers need to develop a feeling for shadows,

Lighting from behind the subject reduces it to a silhouette.

Side lighting reveals contours and gives an impression of volume.

and for what they tell us about the form that cast them. We do this anyway, unconsciously assessing the solidity of an object, gauging its form and even its weight by the shadow it casts. Photographs are two-dimensional, but with careful attention to shadows and shading, they can be made to capture the third dimension of space and depth.

Contrast and lighting ratios

If we are indoors on a sunny day, we can distinguish details in bright sunlight outside and in dark corners inside both at once. If we measure the light intensities of such a scene, we find that differences of 10 stops or more present no problem to the eye, even though this means that the brightest point is 1024 times brighter than the darkest point. If we take a photograph of such a scene, the window bleaches out, and the darker areas appear solid black. One of the main functions of artificial lighting is to compress the contrast ratios of a scene to a level within the emulsion's tolerance. An essential part of thinking photographically is to avoid contrast ratios that are too wide. However dramatic they appear to the eye, they usually fail as photographs. Most films can accept a maximum of five stops, but this calls for very accurate exposures. It is safer, and gives more tolerance to any exposure error, to restrict the ratio to three stops, specially if the end result is to be seen as a print. Slides which are seen by transmitted light (e.g. in a projector) have a slightly wider tolerance, due to the brilliance of the light source, and can usually cope with a four or five stop range.

The Pentax ME Super can be used as a light meter to check contrast ratios. Check the scene visually, and observe which are the lightest and the darkest points. Aim the camera at the lightest point, making sure nothing else comes into the viewfinder to confuse the reading, and taking care not to cast a shadow yourself. Take a reading, then repeat the procedure for the darkest point, and then compare the readings. The longer the lens on the camera, the easier this is: a telephoto lens effectively converts the camera into a spot meter.

Landscape

Successful landscape photographs are gratifying, but not easy to take. Many disappointments await the photographer who simply points his camera at a beautiful landscape and shoots away without considering the special problems of this branch of photography. The results are all too often flat and dreary, lacking in depth and a feeling of space. This is partly a question of composition, specially as regards the placing of the horizon. If the horizon is in the middle of the picture, the result is usually uncomfortably symmetrical, unless there is some strong point of interest there. It is more satisfactory to place the horizon well into the top or bottom half of the picture, dividing it into thirds or quarters, with a generous area of either sky or foreground. Sometimes it is effective to leave the horizon out altogether, or have it broken (e.g. with a tree) or to avoid its being too dead horizontal (e.g. have a hill running down from one side to the other).

If the horizon is placed towards the bottom of the picture, most of the shot will probably be taken up with the sky. A large flat expanse of grey or pale blue does not make for dramatic results, so it is worth waiting for a day with interesting cloud formations. Except in very stormy conditions the sky is usually lighter than the foreground, which leads to exposure problems—either the sky being overexposed and bleached out, or the foreground being too dark. Special graduated filters are available to help overcome this: they are used to darken selectively one portion of the picture. Colour shifts can be introduced too, using graduated colour

In landscape photography, the sky is usually more interesting if there are dramatic cloud formations.

filters, amber being one of the most useful as it helps to warm up the sky tones. A polarizing filter can be used when shooting away from the sun, to darken a blue sky without affecting other colours in the shot.

In black and white work, a yellow, orange or red filter darkens the blue tones in the sky, increasing the contrast with white clouds. Any foliage in the scene will also be darkened; to avoid this looking too dense and clogged, it is advisable to use a yellow filter rather than an orange or red. All these filters call for panchromatic film (most black and white film is panchromatic these days), and all work on the principle of lightening the colour of the filter, and darkening opposite colours (e.g. a green filter lightens foliage, but darkens red brickwork). Through-the-lens metering systems can be thrown out by these filters: the correct procedure is to use the manual mode, read off the exposure without the filter in place, and then use the exposure compensation dial to allow for the filter factor as given by the manufacturer (usually inscribed on the filter mount).

If the horizon is placed towards the top of the picture, it is the composition of the foreground which dominates the photograph. An empty foreground is usually best avoided: look for a viewpoint which brings some desirable feature into the foreground, a feature which leads the eye into the picture, and helps to set the scene and convey a sense of depth and scale. Typical examples might be a fence or river crossing the frame diagonally, a bank of wild flowers, a boat on the beach in a seaside scene, or the skeletal shadow of a tree in winter. If using a wide-angle lens with generous depth of field, dramatic results can be had by going right close in to the foreground subject; a longer lens can give a cooler, more detached perspective. Many successful photographs rely on having a strong line to lead the eye into the picture, such as a meandering path or stream that makes a series of zig-zags. Others depend for their success on framing the scene with the branches of a tree, dramatic clouds, or even a flock of birds. These are all compositional devices, but the less obviously they are used, the more subtle and less hackneyed the results will be. All the ingredients of the composition should look as if they belong there, rather than being artificially manoeuvred into place.

Including water in the foreground gives the opportunity to play with reflections, which can transform an ordinary scene into something much more exciting. A lot depends on how still the water is: a completely flat, glass-like surface can act like a mirror. The more the surface is disturbed, the more broken up will be the image in the reflection. If the surface seems too perfectly mirror-like, experiment by throwing in some pebbles, to see if a more interesting effect is produced. A polarizing filter can be used to cut down reflections, and even penetrate below the surface. One of the difficulties of reflections is that the reflected scene tends to be considerably darker than the real one, giving rise to problems of exposure. A graduated filter can help to bring both parts of the scene within manageable lighting ratios.

Lighting is a vital element in any landscape; the form the composition takes depends entirely on the light it is seen in. A low raking light, where each undulation casts its own shadow, brings out the texture and contours of a landscape, and it is in the search for this type of result that most landscape photographers tend to prefer the hours around sunrise and sunset. This is particularly important when trying to differentiate between the foreground, middle distance, and far distance. With a low-level sun, each zone stands out more clearly than with an overhead light which tends to flatten out perspective.

Another advantage of working in the early morning or late afternoon is the speed with which the light changes, offering great variety of effect within a short space of time. In the early mornings there is sometimes mist hanging in the valleys and hollows, giving an eerie and mysterious air to a scene. Dramatic sunsets can light up the sky with rich glowing colours; but to capture these it is usually necessary to underexpose by one or even two stops—easily accomplished on the Pentax ME Super by using the exposure compensation dial. This underexposure will reduce most foreground subjects to a mere silhouette, so it is worth selecting something with an interesting outline.

There are often problems of colour balance when working in mountain scenery if there is a blue sky and snow on the ground. This is because the snow reflects back more blue into the shadows, giving those areas of the snow that lie in shadow an unacceptably blue cast. A skylight filter helps, but these conditions really call for a pale amber filter. The same problems can arise by the sea, where the reflections from the water can throw a blue tinge into the shadows. Another problem associated with strong sunlight is the haze of a hot summer's day, which can degrade the contrast of distant scenes. A skylight filter helps to reduce the effect of haze; and sometimes a polarizing filter can cut through it quite effectively.

The silhouetted tree and the reflections in the lake make areas of tone: in this case, the effect is very placid.

Vigorous swirling lines and menacing clouds often result from the use of a wide-angle lens (20mm).

Architecture

One of the main difficulties of photographing architecture is the problem of converging verticals, which causes the sides of a building to appear to lean. The eye accepts converging horizontals: if you look along a row of railings, the ones nearer appear larger than those further away. But converging verticals strike us as unnatural; even though the top of a building is usually further away than the bottom, we expect to see all the windows as being equally wide. In a camera, the problem is caused by the optical laws governing parallel lines. As long as the camera is square-on to the subject (i.e. the film plane and the subject plane are parallel to each other), then parallel lines remain parallel when they strike the film. But as soon as the camera is tilted to include the top of the building, the film plane is no longer parallel to the subject. It is nearer the subject at the bottom than at the top; and the top, being further away, appears smaller, giving the effect of converging verticals. The wider the angle of the lens, the more extreme this effect is. Once these principles are understood, there are a number of ways round the problem.

The SMC Pentax Shift 28mm f/3.5 is the answer in terms of equipment. It gives the 35mm camera the feature of a rising-front, more usually associated with large-format cameras. Instead of tilting the camera to include the top of a building, the lens can be 'shifted' upwards. The film plane remains vertical, or parallel to the building, and therefore vertical lines appear vertical. A shift lens is a necessary piece of equipment for anybody who photographs buildings frequently. At 28mm, it gives a 75° angle of view, wide enough to include quite tall buildings without having to go too far back. Because of the construction of the lens, it is impossible to retain the automatic meter coupling. The aperture has to be stopped down manually before shooting.

Another way to avoid converging verticals is to raise your viewpoint so there is no need to tilt the camera. This is not always possible, but sometimes you can go up a hill, or gain access to a building opposite. Failing this another technique is to go further away: the further back you go, the less you will have to tilt the camera to get in the top of the building. If you can go far enough back, or use a wide enough angle lens to keep the centre of the image on the horizon, then the verticals will not converge. Of course you then have the problem of half the picture area being foreground. With negative materials the foreground can be cropped out during printing, but this effectively reduces the format to half-frame, with consequent loss of quality for large prints. It is better where possible to make the foreground an integral part of the picture; perhaps a reflection in some water, or flower beds in a garden, or even the shadow of a tree. This is usually easier with a grand country house in beautiful surroundings than with a town house where the foreground tends be made up of tarmac and yellow lines.

If it is impossible to take the building without converging verticals, then it is sometimes more effective to make a virtue of necessity, and make the converging verticals the main feature of the shot. Dramatic effects can be achieved by looking up the facade from right underneath, giving an impression of dizzying height. With some buildings, specially modern skyscrapers of modular design, abstract patterns can be made out of the repetition of units. If the surface of the building is predominantly glass, the

Three ways to tackle the problem of converging verticals.
Above left: you can exaggerate the effect by pointing the
camera directly upwards—this works best in diagonal
compositions. Right: keep the camera horizontal and choose a
high viewpoint. Below: use a shift lens (see page 140).

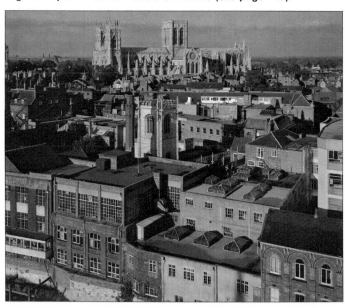

sky can be reflected in the building, so that the edges of the structure appear to dissolve into their surroundings, giving a beautiful effect of translucency and weightlessness. The same type of shot often works well with Gothic buildings, specially interiors, where a cluster of columns soar up into elegant vaulting.

The success of an architectural photograph depends to a large degree on having the right lighting conditions. For a building to appear three-dimensional, sunlight is usually needed—for the maximum feeling of depth it is best to have the sun falling on the facade you are photographing, but from one side, so that each feature like a doorway or window frame casts its own shadow. If your viewpoint includes two sides of a building, and one of these is in shadow, then the contrast between them will convey the sense of depth and mass. But strong sunlight usually means blue skies, which can make every building seem as if it is in the Mediterranean region; so it is often worth waiting for days with interesting cloud formations to avoid this monotonous look.

For more atmospheric shots, you can experiment with different conditions; try shooting into sunsets, or in rainstorms, by night, or even in fog. A rainstorm can leave the ground wet, so that the black surface of a tarmac road becomes reflective. At night many important buildings are floodlit, which offers a convenient way of isolating them from their surroundings. Most floodlighting is nearer to tungsten than daylight in its colour temperature, so for accurate colour rendering (although this is not always necessary), it is preferable to use tungsten-balanced colour film. If in doubt you can take some pictures with the film unfiltered, and some converted to daylight (with a Kodak Wratten Filter no 85B).

Interiors

The problem of long exposures is one of the principal considerations when taking architectural interiors. Most emulsions become less sensitive at slower shutter speeds, and the reciprocity law (see page 23) no longer applies. Most film emulsions are designed to work at shutter speeds of about 1/100; at speeds of 1 second, an extra stop or so is often needed to maintain the correct exposure. With black and white film this 'reciprocity failure' is not too serious; you simply allow the extra time—the details are usually given by the manufacturer's leaflets accompanying the film. But with colour materials it is more serious. Modern colour film is made up of a sandwich, or 'tripack', of three layers of black and white film, each sensitive to one primary colour (red, blue or green). If these three layers have different rates of reciprocity failure, one colour will 'fail' before the others, leading to a colour shift. Colour correction filters can be used to compensate for this, but the filtration required varies from one batch of film to another, adding to the complications. It is more satisfactory to use a film specially intended for long exposures; this usually means one balanced for exposure to tungsten light. These emulsions, often referred to as Type B, are really made for the professional market, but they should be available from specialist retailers. For architectural interiors, where there is an adequate level of natural light, the film should be converted for exposure to daylight with an appropriate filter (e.g. Kodak Wratten 85B filter). Exposures of up to 60 seconds or more give excellent colour rendering using this system.

It is possible to get round this problem by lighting the interiors with

The Gothic Courtyard of the Episcopal Palace, Barcelona, which dates from 1257. These pictures demonstrate two alternative approaches to photographing a building. The picture below was taken with a wide-angle lens to get as much of the courtyard as possible into the picture area. The one on the left shows a detail of the bas-relief on the stairway—a standard or moderate telephoto lens is best for this sort of shot. Display the details alongside the wider views and you have an interesting architectural 'profile'.

flash on daylight film. But even a modest-sized room needs powerful flash equipment, and anything as large as a church really needs several studio flash units, or high-output flash bulbs. So, provided there is enough light, and it is not too uneven, the long exposure system is preferable. Fill-in flash can be used to throw some light into very dark corners; a hand-held flash gun with a fast recycling time can give several flashes during a 30-second exposure. The long exposure system is also likely to give a more natural effect, to give more of the feeling of the architecture. If there is bright sunlight coming through a window, it is best to keep that window out of the shot, as the window will bleach out. As with any photography, it is important to avoid scenes that are too contrasty. Sometimes it is necessary to light the room completely by tungsten light; (the small quartz iodine lamps sold for cine use are particularly good); but to avoid any daylight which would register as blue in a tungsten set-up, it may be necessary to wait until after dark. Some interiors have their own artificial lighting systems, like the floodlighting in a cathedral, and it may be possible to work by this. Under fluorescent tubes use the Pentax FLR filter.

Although tungsten-balanced films avoid the colour shifts caused by 'reciprocity failure', they nevertheless suffer from a loss of film speed, which makes it quite tricky to calculate the correct exposure. Most interior shots need quite a lot of depth of field, so apertures of f/11 or f/16 are often called for. This often pushes the shutter speed into the range of 20 seconds or more.

Most tungsten film is rated at 50 ASA at half a second; at 20 seconds it should be treated as having an effective speed of 16 or 25 ASA (allowing $\frac{1}{3}$ stop for the conversion filter). To obtain meter readings in these low light levels proceed as follows: open the lens fully, with the camera set to manual. Take a reading, e.g. 2 seconds at f/4, and calculate the appropriate exposure for f/11, which works out at 16 seconds. If the meter does not give a reading, you can try the white card method, which relies on the white as being two stops brighter than mid-grey. Take a piece of clean white card or paper, and hold it in front of the lens in such a way that it fills the frame, and is receiving the same sort of illumination as the rest of the scene. If this gives you a reading, calculate the exposure as being two stops more than the white card reading for a normal subject. If the white card reading is 2 seconds at f/4, then a normal exposure would be 8 seconds at f/4; so f/11 would need about one minute—except that reciprocity failure comes in again, so another half stop or so should be given.

A stopwatch is useful for these long exposures, and a tripod is essential, unless a rigid shelf or table top can be found. One feature of these long exposures is that people can walk in and out of the shot: provided they keep moving, and are not too brightly dressed, they do not register on the film. But beware of other photographers with flashguns.

Most interiors call for a wide-angle lens, and since the problem of converging verticals arises as much with interiors as with exteriors, the SMC Pentax Shift 28mm f/3.5 is the ideal tool for most general views. Fish-eye shots can be very effective, specially in confined conditions. Try to make the distortion look deliberate rather than inevitable, and take care not to appear in the picture by mistake.

Still life

With still life, the secret of success is to have maximum control over the lighting. A professional still life studio has a formidable array of lighting equipment—the photographer might need anything from a single spotlight to light a diamond ring to a bank of overhead diffused lights to photograph a new car. Meticulous care is taken over the quality of light, and a lot of effort is put into carefully controlling the degree and density of shadows, and the brilliance of highlights and reflections.

There are two types of equipment, tungsten and flash. The flash is a far cry from the small handy guns that fit into the camera hot shoe; it is usually mains-operated, with a modelling lamp to allow the photographer to assess its effect. There are several advantages of flash for the professional. There is no danger of a blurred picture due to camera shake or subject movement; the lamps do not generate much heat, so they do not cause discomfort to models or risk damaging fragile objects; the low running temperatures also mean they can be incorporated into enclosed diffusing systems (so called fish-fryers), which are specially useful for overhead lighting. The light output can be reduced over a range of settings without affecting colour temperature; and the light is the same colour as daylight, so any daylight appearing in the shot will look quite natural. But some photographers prefer to use tungsten lighting equipment. Its advantages are its lower initial cost, and its lighter weight if it needs to be transported. There is no risk of any discrepancy between the modelling lights and the flash light, so shadows can be assessed exactly. To increase the output of tungsten lighting, you simply take a longer exposure; whereas unless flash has a very high output you may have to work at wide apertures, with consequent problems of depth of field.

For amateur use, tungsten is generally preferable for still life. A basic system of three lights, with a variety of spots and reflectors, can be acquired for less than the cost of a lens. For the owner of the Pentax ME Super, a decisive advantage is that the TTL meter will work perfectly well with tungsten lighting, whereas flash systems need special meters. If you are working in colour, you will have to obtain tungsten-balanced film, and allow for reciprocity failure (see above) at long exposures.

Most lighting systems aim at controlling the shadows, particularly at avoiding shadows that go in opposite directions, as these always look unnatural. Completely shadowless lighting depends on having well diffused light sources as near the camera as possible; in this way, the shadows that are cast are hidden by the subject itself. But completely shadowless lighting can often look rather dull and flat; a soft shadow can be cast by having a diffused light to one side, while extra sparkle and high-lights can be added by a spotlight or undiffused light. There are various ways of diffusing tungsten lamps, whether photofloods or high intensity quartz iodine. The ideal studio has white walls and ceilings, which allow the light to be bounced off them without affecting the colour, or absorbing too much light. This gives very even, soft lighting. More directional diffuse light can be had by using a white reflector with a baffle to mask the light itself (more typically with photofloods), or by hanging some diffusing material in front of the light. Typical materials are tracing paper and tissue paper: but beware of setting the diffuser on fire by letting it get too close to

Glass can be particularly tricky to photograph. Left: a pressed glass tankard, illuminated by a number of light sources close to the camera, and standing on a transparent material. Below: Dartington glass, carefully if simply arranged. The white background is fully illuminated while the use of black (non-reflective) materials on either side has given the decanters a good solid outline.

the bulb. Dressmaker's lining material (trade name Vilene) is very satis-factory: it is rigid enough to hang straight, it comes in different thicknesses, and is fire-resistant. To keep the diffusing material rigid at the top so that it hangs straight down, modelmaker's balsa strips are the ideal combination of rigidity and light weight, and are easily cut to size. To support the diffuser in front of the lamp, Bowen's of London manufacture an invaluable double-ended clip (The Bo-Clip); one end of the clip holds the diffuser, and the other end clips on to the reflector of the lamp. If reflected light is preferred, an American company called Rosco-Gel manufacture a range of reflective materials, which give the effect of the professional's silver umbrellas. The lights are pointed away from the subject, and the reflectors hung in front of them, bouncing a very even light back on to the subject. They come in a number of different tones: white, gold and silver for different effects, as well as blue for converting tungsten to daylight. Reflectors can be improvised out of tin foil stuck or stapled on to card (the less shiny side is usually preferable). Carefully placed black cards are used to control where the light falls, and where it creates a shadow. These cards, provided they are not too heavy, can also be held in place by Bo-Clips, either on the side of the lamp reflector, to act like 'barn doors', or on their own independent stands.

For the maximum control of lighting, adjustable lighting stands are ideal; they allow the lights to be manoeuvred precisely into position. Some floodlights can be fixed with rubber clamps, so chair backs and step ladders can be made into improvised stands.

The usual procedure when photographing a still life is to build up the lighting step by step: start with a main light, and add fill-in lights as required. To assess what effect each light is having, it is useful to be able to switch the lights on and off individually without having to leave the camera. As with other sorts of photography it is important to keep the lighting ratios within the emulsion's contrast range. Successful lighting comes from experiment and experience. A lot can be learned by studying photographs in magazines and on billboards, and trying to analyse the lighting set-ups used.

A vital consideration when photographing any still life is the sort of background wanted. Some subjects have a natural setting which is appropriate—for instance food is usually photographed in a table setting, or on a stove. But individual objects or small groups often look best when placed on a piece of coloured paper, particularly if the paper is big enough to provide the whole background, without having a 'horizon'. The paper needs to be quite long, specially if the professional look of shading at the top is to be achieved. Coloured mounting papers are available from graphic arts supplies shops, but rolls of professional background paper are preferable for photographing anything of any size (and are available from specialist dealers).

The usual practice is to take a table top as a support; fasten the paper as high as necessary to the wall behind, and allow it come forward in a gradual curve, bringing it to the front of the table top. The further the distance between the subject and the wall, the easier it will be to arrange the lighting; this allows the shadows cast by the subject to be kept off the curved portion of the paper, giving the shadows a distorted look.

An 18th or 19th century rock crystal vase, lit from behind. Compare the unlit background with those on page 213.

Some subjects, specially anything transparent like glass, look best when placed on a sheet of perspex and lit from underneath. If the perspex is thin enough to be flexible, it can be curved up at the back in the same way as background paper; if it is too thin it will tend to sag if the subject is at all heavy. If coloured perspex is used, and a low viewpoint is chosen, there will be strong reflections down into the perspex; if these are unwanted, try a higher viewpoint and experiment with a polarizing filter.

It is advisable to use a long focal length lens for still life, as this has the advantage of giving the subject a more natural perspective, and the narrower angle of view reduces the amount of background paper needed to provide a comfortable margin.

Highlights and reflections

There are various ways of removing excessive highlights. Dulling spray can be used, provided it can be cleaned off without damaging the object, or highlights can be daubed with putty. A polarizing filter will remove reflections in one plane from non-metallic surfaces. Very shiny objects like silver are usually placed inside a tent made of some suitable diffuser (Vilene, or a clean white sheet), which is lit from outside, with a small opening for the camera. The tent can be combined with the perspex sheet to give very even lighting, reducing highlights and shadows to a minimum. Or highlights can be given emphasis with a star filter, although this tends to degrade the rest of the image. Other special effect filters used in the still life studio include diffusers for a soft effect, graduated filters to shade the top of the picture, amber and blue filters to warm up or cool down an image, or even a sepia filter to recreate the look of a Victorian photograph. If you do your own printing, you can experiment with montage to superimpose images on top of one another.

Copying

Successful copy photography depends on completely even lighting, control over contrast, and on keeping the camera square to the subject. Special Pentax copying stands are available (see page 143), or an enlarger can be converted; but for occasional use a tripod is good enough for most applications. A small spirit level can be used to ensure that the camera and subject are exactly parallel.

If the subject is glazed, like a painting in a frame, a long lens is useful: the further away the lens from the glass, the less danger there is of reflections. As a safety precaution, a large piece of black card can be placed to mask the camera, with a hole for the lens. This is particularly recommended if the

Title page of Thomas Dekker's 'His Dream', 1620 edition. Note the scale on the left, which could be cropped away if a decorative print were required, but which provides valuable information for reference.

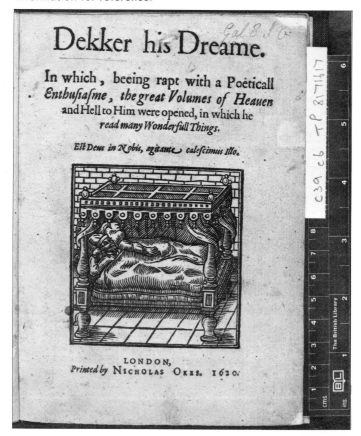

shiny parts of the camera body catch the light. Ideally a flat lens should be used, to avoid 'bellying' or rounding of the image at the edges. The SMC Pentax Macro lenses are specially designed for this, the longer 100m one being particularly useful for avoiding reflections.

When copying documents or photographic prints, it is essential to get the original as flat as possible. A masking frame, as used in enlarging, can be useful for holding the edges down; or a sheet of glass can be used to press the original flat. Pages of old books often have heavy print showing through from the back: in this case a sheet of black card or paper placed behind the page will cut down the 'ghost' image.

The lighting must be as even as possible; two or even four lights should be used. The further away the lights can be placed the more even the result will be—as a rule of thumb, with two lights, the distance from the lights to the centre of the subject should be three times the length of the subject. For example, if a page is 30cm long, each light should be at least 90cm away. A tape measure is useful for checking this. The lighting should be free of hotspots: a flashgun or photoflood in a reflector is an ideal source. To avoid reflections, the lights should be at between 30° and 45° from the subject, and care must be taken to avoid casting any shadow into the surface. Once the lighting is set up, you can check whether it is even by pointing a pencil or finger at the centre of the image: if the shadows on either side are not equally dense, then the lighting is not even. If the subject is an oil painting, it is wise to use a polarizing filter to eliminate highlights picked up by uneven parts of the surface (e.g. ridges of paint).

Copying tends to increase contrast. In black and white the contrast can be controlled to yield a satisfactory negative with detail in both dark and light areas. In colour, it is more a matter of accurate exposure. Except with very dark subjects it is better to underexpose than overexpose; if the results are critical, it is best to do a series of exposures.

Close-up and macro photography

Close-up photographs of nature constitute one of the most rewarding subjects to tackle. Working at close quarters, the camera can reveal textures and pick out details that the naked eye fails to notice. To capture these successfully on film, one or two items of special equipment are needed. A macro lens is ideal, but the standard SMC Pentax lenses can be made suitable for close-up work with close-up lenses, or with extension tubes, or bellows. If non-macro lenses are used, a better optical result may be obtained by reversing the lens (with a reverse adaptor), as this keeps the back element working close to its point of focus; but this naturally uncouples the iris from the metering system. (Pentax Accessories for close up photography are listed on pages 141-144.)

In the Pentax ME Super the light meter takes care of exposure problems caused by the loss of light due to the increased distance from lens to film; but if working with flash, this loss of light must be allowed for.

At these close distances depth of field is very shallow, so it is often advisable to use a fast film to allow the aperture to be as small as possible. The depth of field can be accurately assessed on the ME Super by pressing the lens release button, and turning the lens as if removing it: the lens will then stop down as you look through the camera.

One of the great problems of most natural subjects is that they are mobile: insects walk or fly, and flowers wave about in the wind. Electronic flash can be used to freeze movement; for very even lighting the Pentax AF-080C ring flash can be fitted around the lens. If the subject is more than a few inches from its background, then the background will receive proportionally much less of the flash, and will probably appear dark or even black. This can be a useful way of making a subject stand out very clearly from its background.

If the subject is stable enough to be photographed by available light, then the background will appear (depending also on the depth of field), and these subjects can be shown in their habitat. A low, ground-level tripod is useful, but some workers prefer to use a so-called bean bag, which can be squashed into any desired shape to support the camera. Small flowers can be protected from the wind by erecting a wind break, or they can be steadied with bits of wire stuck in the ground, to which they are

A macro lens has been used to good effect to capture this pattern of larva trails in a dead tree—a rare instance of Dutch elm disease producing something worthwhile.

temporarily fixed with tie-wire closures. Working with available light may cause problems of shutter speed or depth of field, but it is often an important part of the photograph to show what type of environment the subject is to be found in, and for this, flash is usually unsuitable.

For microscopic photography, the Microscope Adaptor K allows the Pentax ME Super body to be fitted to a suitable microscope. Preparing microscopic slides is fascinating but skilled work, although slides can be purchased already prepared. Some types of subjects should be lit from below by the microscope's internal light (tungsten film is usually needed), while others are better lit by reflected light. Some device for stopping down the microscope is a help, to get as much depth of field as possible. With these types of continuous light, the camera's meter will work out the exposures accurately. If the subjects are living, some system of flash can be arranged, but exposures will be a matter of trial and error, the exposure being determined by the distance from the flash to the subject.

Close-up of a beetle, taken with a standard lens fitted with two extension tubes from a set of three. Even at small apertures depth of field is shallow in close-up photography.

35mm films

Conventional colour negative, colour reversal and black and white negative films are commonly available from many manufacturers. Speeds of up to 400 ASA are not unusual, and for low-light photography it is often possible to expose such films at 800 ASA and give them a longer development time—consult your dealer if you do not process your own film at home.

For those who enjoy experimenting with unconventional materials, and those who like creating photographs by the imaginative use of slide copiers, some of the films described below may be of interest.

The following points should be borne in mind.

1. This is not a comprehensive list—it contains only films considered to be of potential interest to the non-specialist amateur.

2. While film speeds and recommended filters are given in some cases, the manufacturers' leaflets should *always* be studied.

3. Where films are available in bulk lengths only, they have to be loaded by the user into re-usable cassettes. This is best accomplished with a bulk film loader.

Colour negative film

Kodak Vericolor Internegative Film 6011: For producing colour negatives from colour transparencies—suitable for use with slide copiers (among other applications). Balanced for tungsten lighting. Available in 80ft rolls for 35mm users.

Colour reversal films

Kodak Ektachrome Infrared Film: For transparencies in which the colours are not those of the original subject. Can be used for surreal or otherwise creative effects; the results are interesting but it cannot be guaranteed that they will always be agreeable. Enthusiasts who persist with this material can obtain some very bizarre photographs. Balanced for daylight with a deep yellow filter. Available in 35mm cassettes only.

Kodak Ektachrome Slide Duplicating Film 5071: A low-contrast film especially designed to cope with the problems of making high-quality duplicate slides (with conventional films, contrast tends to become exaggerated on duplication). Balanced for tungsten lighting. Available in 100ft lengths for 35mm users.

Kodak Vericolor Slide Film 5072: For making colour slides from colour negative originals, by means of a slide copier. Balanced for tungsten lighting. Available in 100ft lengths for 35mm users.

Black and white reversal film

Agfa Dia Direct: A fine-grain film which gives high-quality black and white transparencies for projection. This is a process-paid material which must be returned to the manufacturer's processing stations, the addresses of which are given in the accompanying leaflet; it is normally returned unmounted. Rated at 32 ASA. Available in 36-exposure cassettes.

Black and white negative films

Kodak Recording Film 2475: An ultra-high-speed film; it produces contrasty results with little shadow detail, but it can be rated at 4000 ASA. (Set your camera, when empty, to 4000 ASA and take a few exposure measurements in dim light: this will give you some idea of what Recording Film can do). Designed for specialized technical work, this film is a source of inspiration to many black and white enthusiasts. Available in 35mm cassettes only.

Kodak High-Speed Infrared Film: Another film with serious scientific application but which can be used creatively (see page 78). Living matter such as green foliage comes out white, while blue skies are black. N.B. A deep red filter should be fitted, and the orange focusing index (to the left of the regular focusing index in SMC Pentax lenses) substituted once subject distance has been established. Available in 35mm cassettes.

Ilford XPI 400: A relatively new film, which uses colour-dye technology to combine fine grain with high film speed (400 ASA). Available as a Discovery Kit consisting of one cassette of 35mm film together with the chemicals required to process it. Film and chemicals are also available separately.

Photographic Acknowledgements

Colour
All the photographs in the Sport Section on pages 92-99 were supplied by **Leo Mason**.
All the photographs in the Architecture Section on pages 152-159 were supplied by **Angelo Hornak**.
All the photographs in the Technical Section on pages 172-176 were supplied by **Interfoto Archives**.
T. Brainsbury 110; **John Garrett** 81, 82b, 83, 84t, 84b, 85t, 87, 91b, 100, 106, 107b, 112, 145, 146t, 147t; **Hamlyn Group Picture Library** 111, 151t, 160, 163b, 166, 168, 169; **Don Honeyman** 82t; **Angelo Hornak** 149, 170, 171; **Image Bank** 104t, 104b, 105; **Interfoto Archives** 85b, 90, 146b, 147b, 148, 150t, 150b, 151b, 161t, 162t, 162b, 163t, 165b, 167; **N.H.P.A.—Stephen Dalton** 161b; **N.H.P.A.—Peter Johnson** 164; **N.H.P.A.—S. Robinson** 165t; **Mike Peters** 89, 109; **Scaioni's Studio** 102, 103; **Vloo/Scaioni** 86, 88b, 91t, 101, 108.

Black and White
Catherine Blackie 199l, 199r; **British Museum** 216; **Martin Brown** 43, 44, 68; **Chris Childs** 195; **Peter Crump** 40, 127, 131, 206l, 219; **Dartington Glass** 213b; **Geoff du Feu** 31l, 31r, 42, 114; **John Garrett** 13, 29, 37l, 37r, 63, 70r, 133l, 133r, 183, 185, 186l, 186r, 191b, 198; **Hamlyn Group Picture Library** 22, 210t, 210b, 213t, 215; **Angelo Hornak** 119l, 132, 203l, 203r, 204, 208tl, 208tr, 208b; **Interfoto Archives** 9l, 9r, 17tl, 27, 30, 60, 66, 67, 70l, 118, 119, 125t, 125b, 134, 137, 140, 193l, 195r, 197t, 201l, 201r; **Peter Lemin** 17b, 26, 52, 65, 197b, 218; **L.A.S.L.** 136; **Peter MacDonald** 7, 181, 18r, 25, 32, 74, 77, 78, 128, 130, 206r; **Ian Muggeridge** 135; **Ken Pilsbury** 17tl, 35, 45, 76, 139, 143; **Scaioni's Studio** all photographs on pages 56, 181 & 184, 189, 191tl; **Vloo/Scaioni** 191tr.

Line drawings by **Hayward Art Group**

Jacket acknowledgements
Left **Chris Childs**; centre **Hamlyn Group**; right **John Garrett**.
Back **Hamlyn Group**

The publishers have made every attempt to contact the owners of the illustrations appearing in this book. In the few instances where they have been unsuccessful, they invite the copyright holders to contact them direct.

Index

Main or important subject entries
have page numbers in **bold type**